Asiapac Comics

The Complete
ANALECTS OF CONFUCIUS

論語 孔子

Volume 1

Illustrated by Jeffrey Seow
Paraphrased by Xu Hui
Translated by Adam Sia

ASIAPAC • SINGAPORE

Publisher
ASIAPAC BOOKS PTE LTD
996 Bendemeer Road #06-09 Singapore 339944
Tel: (65) 6392 8455 Fax: (65) 6392 6455
Email: asiapacbooks@pacific.net.sg

Visit us at our Internet home page
www.asiapacbooks.com

First published June 1997
5th edition April 2005

© 1997 ASIAPAC BOOKS, SINGAPORE
ISBN 981-3068-72-8

Bibliographic Data
```
LDR        nam a    00
001        ASP1001
005        20011009104112.0
008        011006s1997    si a          000 0 eng d
020        ≠a9813068728 (pbk.)
041   1    ≠aengchi≠hchi
043        ≠aa-cc---
050   14   ≠aPL2478≠b.L3 S46 1997
082   0    ≠a181.112≠221
100   1    ≠aSeow, Jeffrey.
245   14   ≠aThe complete analects of Confucius /≠cillustrated by
           Jeffrey Seow ; paraphrased by Xu Hui ; translated by Adam
           Sia.
260        ≠aSingapore :≠bAsiapac,≠cc1997.
300        ≠a377 p. :≠bchiefly ill. ;≠c21 cm.
440   0    ≠aAsiapac comic series
546        ≠aText in English and Chinese.
650   0    ≠aConfucianism≠vCaricatures and cartoons.
700   1    ≠aXu, Hui.
700   1    ≠aSia, Adam.
700   0    ≠aConfucius.≠tLun y-u.≠lEnglish & Chinese.
```

Cover illustration by Jeffrey Seow
Cover design by Illusion Creative Studio
Body text in 8pt Comic Sans
Printed in Singapore by Loi Printing Pte Ltd

CONTENTS

Volume One

About the Illustrator
About the Interpreter
About the Translator
Publisher's Note
Preface by Dr Lee Cheuk Yin
The Main Disciples of Confucius Featured in the Analects

ABOUT THE ILLUSTRATOR

Jeffrey Seow, a self taught artist, is best known for *The Wonder Kids*〈〈小和尚〉〉, a pictorial series, popularly seen on bookmarks and other collectibles. Prior to his foray into comic books production, Jeffrey worked for six years in the local TV station, and 15 years in the advertising industry. His works during this period include story-boards, illustrations for books, as well as animation. These attest to his versatility and creativity.

He presently works on a freelance basis, continuing to expand his repetoire of artistic works. A number of Jeffrey's works, are imbued with a deep sense of morality. The vividness each principles he portrays in his cartoon characters can only stem from his own belief that life should be ordered around the practice of such values.

The value of entertainment and moral cultivation has been proven to be a great attraction of his series *The Wonder Kids*. In *The Complete Analects of Confucius*, he has adopted the same approach to demonstrate his practical appreciation of Confucius' teachings.

ABOUT THE INTERPRETER

Xu Hui majored in Chinese Literature and Linguistics in Southwest Normal University (China). Spurred on by her interest in education, she became lecturer of Chinese language and ancient literature in Chongqing Architectural University.

She is the writer and editor of several educational titles in the Chinese Language, and is the author of *Golden Rules for Business Success* published by Asiapac Books.

ABOUT THE TRANSLATOR

Adam Sia majored in English Language and Sociology at the National University of Singapore. After his graduation he became an in-house writer at a local publishing firm.

The pragmatic view he adopts when looking at his Chinese heritage has enabled him to write a series of practical self-help comic books, including *The Chinese A.R.T. of Goal Setting*, *The Chinese T.A.C.T.I.C in Negotiation*, *The Chinese Art of Leadership* and *The Chinese Art of Excellence* published by Asiapac Books.

PUBLISHER'S NOTE

Confucius is indeed a great sage who has left a legacy of works behind that continues to impact every aspect of life in the modern age. Therefore it is with great pleasure that Asiapac brings to you this new edition of *The Analects* in its full extent.

Unlike most other philosophical works which have a didactic tone, *The Analects* conveys the tenets of Confucius' teachings by describing the actions of the sage in his daily life. *The Analects*, compiled by Confucius' disciples who each saw their master from a different perspective, offers a complete picture of the person of Confucius. For this reason, the Confucius we see in this edition of *The Analects* is affable yet stern, profound yet down to earth. This dismisses the stiff and stuffy images that many associate with the benign sage.

We would like to take this opportunity to thank Dr Lee Cheuk Yin for writing an insightful preface of the *Analects* for us, Jeffrey Seow for bringing to life the person of Confucius with his vivid drawings and the production team for their contributions to the publication of this book.

Other Asiapac Comics on Confucius

- *THE SAYINGS OF CONFUCIUS* by Tsai Chih Chung (Extracts from *Lun Yu-The Analects*)
- *THE WISDOM OF CONFUCIUS* by Tsai Chih Chung (Extracts from *Da Xue-The Great Learning and Zhong Yong-The Doctrine of the Mean*)

PREFACE

The greatest influence that China's two thousand years long history had came from the Confucianism. And for the Confucian school of thought, the *Confucian Analects* represents its most important work. Since the Southern Song Dynasty (1127-1279) until the Qing Dynasty (1644-1911), the *Analects*, along with the *Book of Mencius*, the *Great Learning* and the *Doctrine of the Mean* (also known as the *Four Books*), has been made required readings for scholars intending to sit for the civil service examinations.

The *Analects* was first introduced to Europe by missionaries who arrived in China during the 16th century. Currently, the *Analects* is available in English, French, German, Latin, Italian, Japanese, Spanish and Malay among many other languages. This enabled the *Analects* to make an indelible impact internationally. Some have even gone to the extent of referring to the *Analects* as the bible of Confucianism.

The *Analects* is a record of the life and sayings of Confucius. Ban Gu in *The Standard History of the Han Dynasty* said that the *Analects* is "a record of Confucius' answers and his conversations with his disciples and his contemporaries". After Confucius' death, his students compiled his sayings into a book thereby creating the *Confucian Analects*.

Confucius, a latinized name given by the Europeans, was born in BC 551 and died in BC 479. His family name was Kong and his personal name Qiu. He lived in the State of Lu (present day Qufu in Shantong Province) and descended from a line of aristocrats. His father served as an official of the State of Lu. Confucius' father died when he was only three, leaving him with an impoverished childhood. But he was a diligent and inquisitive child who had a drive to improve himself. Soon he became well versed in ancient literature and gained a good grasp of the subjects he studied.

He broke the monopoly the aristocrats had over education by setting up a private institution of learning which enrolled students from all walks of life and through this, popularized education. For this reason, Confucius was revered posthumously as the "Sage of Teachers". When he was 47, Confucius became a steward of the central capital and governed the district of Qufu. Later he was promoted to the position of Minister of Works and Minister of Justice. When he was 54, he became the Acting Grand Councillor of Lu. However, during that period, the ruler indulged in entertainment and neglected the affairs of the state. Disillusioned by this, Confucius left the State of Lu and led his students on a tour of the states, proselytising to the feudal lords, as they travelled, his philosophy of governance. In this voyage, he visited seven states including Wei, Zhao, Song, Zheng, Cheng, Cai and Chu. After 14 years, when Confucius was already 68, he returned to the State of Lu, and committed himself to editing and teaching the ancient classics.

Confucius lived during the end of the Spring and Autumn Period (B.C. 770-B.C. 476). This was a period when the Zhou Dynasty declined and feudal lords occupied the states. War and anarchy reigned throughout the land. It was a time when the rites was disregarded, musical regulations flouted and chaos reigned. Confucius preached the idea of benevolence, hoping to bring some changes to the politically and socially unsettling period.

Confucius' political philosophy is based on the moral training of individuals. He encouraged each person to see to his own cultivation of benevolence and through the practice of this, to gradually influence others. In the *Analects*, Confucius gives a concise and succinct explanation of benevolence (ren) as a concept. He said: "Love your fellow men." He advocates the principle of "do not do to others what you do not wish to be done to yourself" and "desiring to sustain oneself, one sustains others; desiring to develop oneself, one develops others." Confucius believed that if the ruler and the masses would practise benevolence, it would result in peace for the country and harmony in society. In this way we can see how the ideal of benevolence is a core value in Confucius' teachings. It is this fundamental value that has laid for future generations of Confucianists, a foundation and framework to further explore the philosophy of Confucianism.

In the *Analects* of Confucius, another frequently mentioned idea is propriety or the rites (li). For Confucius, the idea of benevolence and the rites are inseparable. The word "benevolence" appears 109 times and the word "rites" appear 75 times in the *Analects*. Often these two words are treated as a single entity. The rites refers to the regulations and customs followed by those who lived during the primordial period. When Confucius' disciple Yan Yuan asked for a definition of benevolence, Confucius answered: "To regulate oneself and follow the rites is to be benevolent", "If it does not conform to the rites, do not look; if it does not conform to the rites, do not listen; if it does not conform to the rites, do not speak; if it does not conform to the rites, do not take action". From this, one can see that adherence to the rites, is the means to be benevolent. When questioned about "filial piety", Confucius' explanation was, "When your parents are alive, comply with the rites in loving them; when they die, comply with the rites in burying them; comply with the rites in sacrificing to them." In Confucian thought, benevolence and the rites can be regarded respectively as the principle and the methodology. Correspondingly to this, benevolence may be regarded as the main idea and the rites, a secondary idea.

The *Analects* covers a wide range of topics, giving a full exposition on politics, society, morality, education, literature and the arts among others, making this book the most important literary work for understanding Confucius' thoughts. All these factors, including the conciseness and poetry of the language used, the depth of meaning and the conversational style in which the ideas are presented, makes the *Analects* a book of such richness and vividness, that once read is difficult to forget.

In recent years we see a trend towards reinterpreting classical Chinese literature for modern living. With this, the *Analects* of Confucius has found renewed relevance and prominence in the commercial world. Chibuzawa Eiichi (1840-1931), who is known as the father of enterprise in Japan, wrote *The Analects and the Abacus*, which applies his findings and experiences with the *Analects* to business and management. This is a testimony to the depth of knowledge contained in the *Analects*, its extensive coverage and practicality. The timelessness of the Analects demonstrated through this interpretation also attests to the value of this great work.

In order to allow more people to have a deeper understanding of the *Analects*, Asiapac Books of Singapore has specially produced a Chinese-English edition of this great work, accompanied by cartoon illustrations of each saying. This new medium of presenting this ancient classical Chinese text is an effort to further simplify and popularize this classical text for readers. It will not only aide the further development of Confucianism but will also prove to be beneficial for society.

Dr Lee Cheuk Yin
Department of Chinese Studies
National University of Singapore

THE MAIN DISCIPLES OF CONFUCIUS
FEATURED IN THE ANALECTS

Family Name: Yan   姓   :颜
Given Name : Yan Hui   名   :颜回
Styled Name: Zi Yuan   字   :子渊
Other Name : Yan Yuan   外称:颜渊

Family Name: Min   姓   :闵
Given Name : Min Sun   名   :闵损
Styled Name: Zi Qian   字   :子骞
Other Name :   ---   外称 : ---

Family Name: Ran   姓   :冉
Given Name : Ran Geng   名   :冉耕
Styled Name: Bo Niu   字   :伯牛
Other Name :   ---   外称 : ---

Family Name: Ran   姓   :冉
Given Name : RanYong   名   :冉雍
Styled Name: Zhong Gong 字   :仲弓
Other Name :   ---   外称 : ---

Family Name: Zai   姓   :宰
Given Name : Zai Yu   名   :宰予
Styled Name: Zi Wo   字   :子我
Other Name : Zai Wo   外称:宰我

Family Name: Duanmu   姓　：端木
Given Name : Ci   名　：賜
Styled Name: Zi Gong   字　：子貢
Other Name : ---   外称：---

Family Name: Ran   姓　：冉
Given Name : Qiu   名　：求
Styled Name: Zi You   字　：子由
Other Name : Ran You   外称：冉由

Family Name: Zhong   姓　：仲
Given Name : You   名　：由
Styled Name: Zi Lu   字　：子路
Other Name : Ji Lu   外称：季路

Family Name: Yan   姓　：言
Given Name : Yan   名　：偃
Styled Name: Zi You   字　：子游
Other Name : ---   外称 : ---

Family Name: Bu   姓　：卜
Given Name : Shang   名　：商
Styled Name: Zi Xia   字　：子夏
Other Name : ---   外称：---

Family Name: Zhuansun　姓　　:颛孙
Given Name : Shi　　　 名　　:师
Styled Name: Zi Zhang　字　　:子张
Other Name : ---　　　 外称 : ---

Family Name: Zeng　　 姓　:曾
Given Name : Shen　　 名　:参
Styled Name: Zi Yu　　 字　:子舆
Other Name: Zeng Zi　 外称:曾子

Family Name: Gong　　 姓　:公
Given Name : Xichi　　 名　:西赤
Styled Name: Zi Hua　　字　:子华
Other Name : Gong Xihua 外称:公西华

Family Name: Fan　 姓　:樊
Given Name : Xu　　名　:须
Styled Name: Zi Chi　字　:子迟
Other Name: Fan Chi　外称:樊迟

Family Name: Zeng　　 姓　:曾
Given Name : Dian　　 名　:点
Styled Name: Zi Xi　　 字　:子皙
Other Name : Zeng Xi　外称:曾皙

The Complete
ANALECTS
of Confucius
Volume 1

学而篇第一
Chapter One, Xue Er

1.

【原文】

子曰:"学而时习之, 不亦说乎? 有朋自远方来, 不亦乐乎? 人不知, 而不愠, 不亦君子乎?"

【译文】

孔子说:"常常去实习自己学过的知识, 不是很好的事吗? 有朋友从远方来, 不是很高兴的事吗? 不因为别人不了解自己而抱怨, 不是很有修养的君子风度吗?"

【English Translation】

Confucius said: "Regarding the new knowledge one learns, isn't it a joy to put it into practice in due time? When friends come to visit from afar, isn't it a great delight? Isn't not harbouring ill feelings over the inability of others to look up to oneself a gentlemanly attribute?"

2.

【原文】

有子曰:"其为人也孝弟, 而好犯上者, 鲜矣; 不好犯上, 而好作乱者, 未之有也。君子务本, 本立而道生。孝弟也者, 其为仁之本与?"

【译文】

有子说:"孝顺父母、敬爱兄长的人, 却喜欢触犯上司, 这种人是很少见的; 从不触犯上司, 却喜造反作乱, 这种人从来没有过。君子致力于"根本"的树立, 根本树立了, 治国做人的原则就会产生。孝顺父母, 敬爱兄长, 就是仁爱的根本吧!"

【English Translation】

You Zi said: "It is difficult is find someone who is filial towards his parents; respectful to elders but yet fond of rebelling against authorities. There has been none who is fond of causing trouble but not fond of offending their superiors. The gentleman turns his attention toward building up the basics. Once that is done, his philosophy of life would have been found. To be filial towards one's parents and to respect one's elders, this is the root of benevolence."

You Zi

Few indeed are those who respect their elders but love to offend those in authority.

A person who is keen to start a rebellion but careful not to offend his elders is almost non-existent!

The principles of government stem from the basics.

The basis of government and good behaviour is filial piety and respect for elders.

5

3.

【原文】
子曰:"巧言令色,
鲜矣仁!"

【译文】
孔子说:"花言巧语,伪装和善的人,
不会有什么仁德。"

【English Translation】
Confucius said: "Those with a glib tongue
and who pretends to look respectable
lacks loving kindness."

Those with a glib tongue.

And who pretend to be kind.

Here's a little spending money.

Do not have benevolence.

Give me my money back WITH INTEREST!

4

【原文】

曾子曰:"吾日三省吾身: 为人谋而不忠乎? 与朋友交而不信乎? 传不习乎?"

【译文】

曾子说:"我每天都再三反省自己: 为别人办事是否尽心尽力了? 同朋友交往是否以诚相待了? 老师传授的学业是否用心复习了?"

【English Translation】

Zeng Zi: "Daily, I examine myself in three areas. Have I taken advantage of others? Have I been unfaithful to my friends? Have I put into practice the lessons I have learnt?"

9

5.

【原文】

子曰:"道千乘之国, 敬事而信,
节用而爱人, 使民以时。"

【译文】

孔子说:"治理一个拥有兵车千乘的国家,
处理政事要慎重, 办事要讲信用,
节省开支, 爱护官吏,
差遣百姓要不误农时。"

【English Translation】

Confucius said: "When ruling a country
with a thousand chariots, one must be respectable
and trustworthy, exercise economy and
affection to subjects and employ the people
only at the proper seasons."

6.

【原文】

子曰:"弟子，入则孝，出则悌，谨而信，泛爱众而亲仁。行有余力，则以学文。"

【译文】

孔子说:"年轻人在家要孝顺父母，在外要敬爱兄长，做事谨慎认真，说话诚实守信，博爱大众亲近有仁德的人。有时间就要学习文化知识。"

【English Translation】

Confucius said: "A youth should be filial when at home and respectful towards the elders when abroad; faithful in deeds and truthful in words. He should love everyone but draw close only to those who demonstrate benevolence. Should he have energy to spare, let him spend it on the polite arts."

7.

【原文】

子夏曰:"贤贤易色;事父母,能竭其力;事君,能致其身;与朋友交,言而有信。虽曰未学,吾必谓之学矣。"

【译文】

子夏说:"对妻子,重品德不重容貌;事奉父母,能尽心尽力;为国家能鞠躬尽瘁;与朋友交往诚实而守信。这样的人虽然没有上过学,但我认为他已经学好了。"

【English Translation】

Zi Xia said: "He who pays more attention to character and not beauty, who does his best to serve his parents, devotes his life to serve the country and keeps his promises to his friends, though unschooled, should surely be counted as one among the learned."

A man who values his wife's virtues above her appearance ,...

... serves his parents with his best effort, ...

Reservist

... serves his country with loyalty and ...

... keeps his promises,

I trust you!

... is well educated although he has not been to school.

Are you a scholar?

He's the farmer who lives next door!

8.

【原文】

子曰:"君子不重则不威, 学则不固。主忠信, 无友不如己者。过则勿惮改。"

【译文】

孔子说:"君子不庄重就不威严, 不踏实就学无成就。要重道德, 讲信用, 慎交友; 有过错, 就不要怕改正。"

【English Translation】

Confucius said: "A gentlemen who is frivolous earns no respect. He does not put his mind to studying and can never acquire a grounding in his knowledge. One should learn to be loyal and sincere, and be wary of those who are immoral. If he makes a mistake, he should rectify it promptly."

17

9.

【原文】

曾子曰:"慎终追远,
民德归厚矣。"

【译文】

曾子说:"慎重地办理父母的丧事,虔诚地祭祀祖先,这样做自然会民风淳厚了。"

【English Translation】

Zeng Zi said: "When the funeral rites of deceased parents are practised meticulously and the practice of offering sacrifices to ancestors observed faithfully, the morality of the people will reach its pinnacle."

When funerals are conducted according to the rites,

and sacrifices to distant ancestors given devoutly,

the state of morality will reach a peak.

10.

【原文】

子禽问于子贡曰:"夫子至于是邦也，必闻其政，求之与？抑与之与？"子贡曰:"夫子温、良、恭、俭、让以得之。夫子之求之也，其诸异乎人之求之与？"

【译文】

子禽问子贡说:"孔子每到一个国家，就知道那个国家的政事，是他自己打听到的呢？还是人家主动告诉他的？"子贡说:"他老人家以温和、善良、恭敬，俭朴、谦逊的风范而使人家乐于主动把这个国家的政事告诉他。他这种获悉的方法，不同于别人吧？"

【English Translation】

Zi Qin asked Zi Gong: "Whenever the teacher (Confucius) goes to a foreign country, he always manages to find out about the political situation there. Does he do this by asking questions or do people tell him of their own accord?"

Zi Gong answered: "The teacher gets information by being upright, respectful, temperate and deferential. The teacher's manner of inquiry indeed sets him apart from others."

11.

【原文】

子曰:"父在，观其志；父没，观其行；三年无改于父之道，可谓孝矣。"

【译文】

孔子说:"在他父亲活着的时候看他的志向是否正确，父亲去世后看他的行为是否正确，如果他在父亲去世后三年之内不改变父亲留下的正确原则，就可以说他尽孝了。"

【English Translation】

Confucius said: "When a man's father is alive, check his ideals. When a man's father is deceased, watch his conduct. If for three years after he does not change the ways he observes as when his father was alive, he has fulfilled his duty of filial piety."

23

12.

【原文】

有子曰："礼之用，和为贵。先王之道，斯为美，大小由之。有所不行，知和而和，不以礼节之，亦不可行也。"

【译文】

有子说："礼的应用，以遇事和顺为可贵。从前圣明君主治理国家，可贵之处就在于，他们不管小事大事，都按这条原则去处理。但有时也行不通，那是因为只懂得求和顺，而不知道用礼法去节制约束它，所以就行不通了。"

【English Translation】

You Zi said: "It is most important to seek the balance of harmony in conducting rites. The beauty of the kings in history lies in this, regardless of the severity of the matter, they followed this principle. However, there are situations when harmony must be modulated by rites."

The main objective of rules and rites.

But seeking harmony
without rites does not work.

25

13.

【原文】

有子曰："信近于义，言可复也。恭近于礼，远耻辱也。因不失其亲，亦可宗也。"

【译文】

有子说："信约符合道义，就可以实行。行为合于礼法，就可避免羞耻侮辱。依靠信得过的人，也是可以效法的。"

【English Translation】

You Zi said: "Trustworthiness is akin to righteousness. Promises made will then be kept. Respect has great affinity with propriety which keeps embarrassment and ridicule away. When those whom a person relies upon are proper, one can make them masters and guides."

Promises should be kept.

This is as agreed.

Thank you!

RICE

Respectable behaviour keeps disgrace and insults away.

Shameless lecher!

Sorry, dear!

Rely on those with integrity to find stability.

Want to earn some extra pocket money?

No, thanks!

27

14.

【原文】

子曰："君子食无求饱，居无求安，敏于事而慎于言，就有道而正焉，可谓好学也已。"

【译文】

孔子说："君子吃饭不求饱足，居住不求舒适，办事敏捷，说话谨慎，向有道义学问高的人学习来完善自己，这样就可以说是好学了。"

【English Translation】

Confucius said: "A gentleman does not seek to satiate his appetite or demand luxurious trappings. He is efficient at work, and cautious when speaking; he corrects himself by learning from the accomplished and virtuous. These are the attributes which mark him out to be a keen learner."

29

15.

【原文】

子贡曰:"贫而无谄, 富而无骄, 如何?"子曰: "可也, 未若贫而乐, 富而好礼者也。"

子贡曰:"《诗》云: '如切如磋, 如琢如磨', 其斯 之谓与?"子曰:"赐也, 始可与言《诗》已矣, 告诸往 而知来者。"

【译文】

子贡说:"贫穷而不巴结人, 富贵而不骄傲自大, 这 种人怎么样?"孔子说:"还可以, 但不如那种虽贫穷却仍 然十分快乐, 虽富贵却谦虚好礼的人。"

子贡说:"《诗经》上说: '精雕细刻再打磨光滑, 方 能成器', 做人也一样吧?"

孔子说:"赐呀, 现在可以同你讨论《诗经》了, 告 诉你以前的事, 你可以推断后来的事, 你能举一反三。"

【English Translation】

Zi Gong asked: "What do you think of a person who is poor but does not flatter, rich and yet not haughty?"
Confucius said: "Good but it cannot compare with those who are poor but remain joyful, or rich and yet respectful."

Zi Gong said: "It is stated in the *Book of Songs* that bone and jade require repeated carving before they are polished to a shine. Isn't this what it means?"

Confucius replied: "Oh, Ci (Zi Gong's style name), we are ready to discuss the *Book of Songs* now since you are able to make inferences about the present from the past."

31

16.

【原文】

子曰:"不患人之不己知,
患不知人也。"

【译文】

孔子说:"不怕别人不了解自己,
就怕自己不了解别人。"

【English Translation】
Confucius said: "Do not fret about being
misunderstood but be concerned that you
cannot understand others."

为政篇第二
Chapter Two, Wei Zheng

1.

【原文】

子曰:"为政以德,
譬如北辰居其所而众星共之。"

【译文】

孔子说:"国君如果用道德来治理
国家大事,自己就会像北极星受群星
环绕一样受到百姓拥护。"

【English Translation】

Confucius said: "One who governs with morality
is like the North Star which holds its position
while the other stars pay homage to it."

A monarch who rules with a high standard of morality, ...

... is like the North Star, revered and respected by the surrounding stars.

2.

【原文】

子曰:"《诗》三百,

一言以蔽之,

曰:'思无邪'。"

【译文】

孔子说:"《诗经》三百篇,

用一句话来概括地评价

就是'思想纯正'。"

【English Translation】

Confucius said: "The Book of Poetry contains

three hundred entries, if I had to summarise

the teachings of the book in one sentence,

it would read: 'A pure and untainted mind.' "

3.

【原文】

子曰："道之以政，齐之以刑，民免而无耻；道之以德，齐之以礼，有耻且格。"

【译文】

孔子说："靠行政命令和刑罚来制约百姓，他们只知道避免犯罪受刑罚而不知道犯罪是耻辱的；如果用道德和礼教来引导百姓，他们就会不仅仅知道犯罪是耻辱的，而且还能够自我约束。"

【English Translation】

Confucius said: "Ruling the people with the regulations and achieving obedience through punishment will result in a people who will not break the law but have no self respect.

Ruling the people with moral force and maintaining order through the rules of propriety will result in them coming to you of their own accord and keeping their self respect."

4.

【原文】

子曰:"吾十有五而志于学, 三十而立, 四十而不惑, 五十而知天命, 六十而耳顺, 七十而从心所欲, 不逾距。"

【译文】

孔子说:"我十五岁有志于做学问; 三十岁立身处世; 四十岁掌握了各种知识遇事不迷惑; 五十岁知道上天给予自己的使命; 六十岁对别人说的话能辨别是非曲直; 七十岁可以做到随心所欲而不会有越轨的行为。"

【English Translation】

Confucius said: "When I was fifteen, I aspired to learn. At thirty I found my footing. At forty I cleared all doubts. At fifty I knew the will of heaven. At sixty, I was able to discern the truth. At seventy, I could follow my heart's desires without transgressing what is right."

At 15, I set my mind to acquire knowledge.

At 30, ...

I've found my stand!

I'll handle it.

Your call!

BILL

At 40, I was not disturbed by the contradictions in life.

At 50, I've come to understand heaven's will for me.

At 60, I was able to discern the words of others.

Malicious gossip!

At 70, I felt free to do anything since the law had become a natural part of me.

HA!

HA!

?

5.

【原文】

孟懿子问孝，子曰:"无违。"

樊迟御，子告之曰:"孟孙问孝于我，我对曰，无违。"樊迟曰:"何谓也?"子曰:"生，事之以礼；死，葬之以礼，祭之以礼。"

【译文】

孟懿子请教孔子什么是孝道，孔子说:"不要违背礼节。"

有一次，樊迟为孔子赶车，孔子告诉他说:"孟孙问我孝道是什么，我答复他说，不要违背礼节。"樊迟问:"是什么意思呢?"孔子说:"父母活着的时候，按礼节侍奉他们，父母去世后，按礼节埋葬他们并按礼节祭祀他们。"

【English Translation】

Meng Yi Zi consulted Confucius about filial piety. Confucius said: "Never disobey."

Soon after, when Fan Chi was driving the carriage exclusively for Confucius, the teacher said: "Meng asked me what filial piety was and I told him that it was not being disobedient."

Fan Chi asked: "Why is that so?"

Confucius answered: "When they are alive, serve them according to the rules of propriety; when they are dead, they should be buried and remembered according to the rules of propriety."

6.

【原文】

孟武伯问孝，

子曰："父母唯其疾之忧。"

【译文】

孟武伯请教孔子什么是孝道，

孔子说："特别为父母的疾病担忧。"

【English Translation】

Meng Wubo consulted Confucius about filial piety. Confucius said: "Behave in such a way that your parents have no anxiety about you except with regard to your health."

What is filial piety?

What am I to do?

To be concerned about the health of one's parent is to be filial.

45

7.

【原文】

子游问孝。子曰:"今之孝者，是谓能养。至于犬马，皆能有养。不敬，何以别乎?"

【译文】

子游请教孔子什么是孝道。孔子说:"现在的孝道，只是说能够供养父母就行了。就是犬马，也能做到这一点。如果心里对父母不存孝敬之情，那和犬马有什么区别呢?"

【English Translation】

Zi You consulted Confucius about filial piety. Confucius said: Those who are filial in our day see to the physical needs of their parents. Even dogs and horses get the same. How is one's treatment of parents different from these animals, if one does not show his parents respect?

8.

【原文】

子夏问孝。子曰:"色难。有事, 弟子服其劳; 有酒食, 先生馔。曾是以为孝乎?"

【译文】

子夏请教孔子什么是孝道, 孔子说:"对父母经常保持和颜悦色最难。有事情的时候, 儿子为父母效劳; 有酒食的时候, 让父母吃喝。难道做到这些就算孝吗?"

【English Translation】

Zi Xia consulted Confucius about filial piety.

Confucius said: "To serve one's parents with a joyful countenance on one's face is most difficult. Running errands whenever necessary, sharing one's food and wine, can this amount to being filial?"

To merely share food and drink with one's parents can hardly be called filial piety.

It's most difficult to serve with a joyful expression constantly.

9.

【原文】

子曰:"吾与回言终日，不违，如愚。退而省其私，亦足以发，回也不愚。"

【译文】

孔子说:"我整天和颜回讲学，他从来不提反对意见和疑问，好像很愚笨。可是我发现他自己私下钻研时，也有所发挥，可见他并不愚笨。"

【English Translation】

Confucius said: "For the whole day that I spoke to Yan Hui, he did not show any disagreement. This makes him appear stupid. But I discovered that when he is not with me, he demonstrates what I've taught him. This shows that he is not dimwitted after all. "

Do you understand?

That makes sense!

Every time I tutor Yan Hui, all he says is, ...

But when he is studying in private, he does produce profound thoughts.

I've found it!

This proves that he is not stupid at all.

SHHHH!

10.

【原文】

子曰："视其所以，观其所由，察其所安。人焉瘦哉？人焉瘦哉？"

【译文】

孔子说："要了解一个人，要看他的所作所为，既要了解他的过去，又要观察他的现在，这样来了解一个人还会不全面吗？"

【English Translation】

Confucius said: "To understand a person well, observe his actions, find out about his past and watch him when he is relaxed. (relaxed takes the meaning of a Chinese proverb meaning to bear hardship with equanimity). How can a man hide his true self from you then?"

Past

We can know a person by his deeds.

Present

If we can see how his past actions led to the present situation, and how he feels about it, how can we not understand him?

11.

【原文】

子曰:"温故而知新,
可以为师矣。"

【译文】

孔子说:"温习学过的知识
而能获得新知识的人,
可以做老师了。"

【English Translation】

Confucius said: "If one is able to learn new
knowledge by reviewing old knowledge,
he may then be a teacher of others."

12.

【原文】

子曰:"君子不器。"

【译文】

孔子说:"君子不能象俗器一样,
而应有广博的知识。"

【English Translation】

Confucius said: "A gentleman is not like a utensil
(having specific and limited uses)."

A gentleman is knowledgeable in many fields.

13.

【原文】

子贡问君子。

子曰:"先行其言而后从之。"

【译文】

子贡问怎样才能做个君子。

孔子说:"君子总是先实行所想到的事,
然后再说出来。"

【English Translation】

Zi Gong asked about the true gentleman.

Confucius said: "He does not preach what he
practises till he has practised what he preaches."

14.

【原文】

子曰:"君子周而不比,
小人比而不周。"

【译文】

孔子说:"君子团结但不互相勾结,
小人互相勾结而不团结。"

【English Translation】

Confucius said: "The gentleman promotes
unity and does not perpetuate differences;
petty men compare themselves with
one another which destroys unity."

A gentleman promotes unity by being considerate.

Petty men conspire, thereby bringing about segregation and dissension.

61

15.

【原文】

子曰:"学而不思则罔,

思而不学则殆。"

【译文】

孔子说:"只读书不思考,就会感到迷惑。

只空想不读书,就不明事理。"

【English Translation】

Confucius said: "To learn without thinking brings
about ignorance, to think without learning
bring about muddle-headedness."

Some read without thinking.

Some others think without reading, ...

If fishes with tails can swim, then cats with tails can swim too.

He cannot understand and analyse things around him.

... and spout nonsense.

Mumbo Jumbo.

16.

【原文】
子曰:"攻乎异端,
斯害也已。"

【译文】
孔子说:"批判异端邪说,
祸害自然消灭。"

【English Translation】
Confucius said: "Criticize unorthodox ideas
fiercely and it will be eliminated."

In handling unorthodox theories, attack it vehemently.

What he's saying does not make sense!

That's why, it will naturally be eliminated.

17.

【原文】

子曰:"由!诲女知之乎?知之为知之,
不知为不知,是知也。"

【译文】

孔子说:"由啊!我讲的你懂了吗?懂就说懂,
不懂就说不懂,这才是聪明的人。"

【English Translation】

Confucius said: "You! Do you understand what I'm
saying? If you understand it, say that you understand it.
If you do not understand it, say that you do not
understand it. That is true knowledge indeed!"

18.

【原文】

子张学干禄，子曰："多闻阙疑，慎言其余，则寡尤；多见阙殆，慎行其余，则寡悔。言寡尤，行寡悔，禄在其中矣。"

【译文】

子张请教孔子求官的方法，孔子说："多倾听，不讲没把握的话，即使有把握也要谨慎地讲，这样可以少犯错误；多观察，不做没把握的事，即使有把握也要细心去做，这样可以少干错事。不说错话，不干错事，俸禄就在这里面。"

【English Translation】

Zi Zhang sought the advice of Confucius regarding the way to gain an official appointment.

Confucius said: "Listen more and speak less. Be extra cautious when you speak. Take extra caution so as to avoid occasions for blame. Observe more and set aside dubious action. Pay extra attention to your works and you will avoid regret. With fewer slips of the tongue and fewer regrets, official positions can be obtained."

How does one become a good official?

Hear what everyone has to say.

Listen only to the upright.

Observe everything around oneself but only practise what is correct.

Such an honest man!

Those who make fewer mistakes will be appointed officials.

19.

【原文】

哀公问曰："何为则民服？"孔子对曰："举直错诸枉，则民服；举枉错诸直，则民不服。"

【译文】

鲁哀公问孔子："怎样做才能让百姓信服呢？"孔子回答说："选用正直的人，压制邪恶的人，老百姓就会信服；选用邪恶的人，而压制正直的人，老百姓就不会信服。"

【English Translation】

Duke Ai of Lu enquired of Confucius: How does one win the trust and submission of the people?

Confucius said: "Promote the upright and suppress the wicked, to get the obedience of the people. If the wicked are raised up and the upright suppressed, the people will not submit to your authority."

20.

【原文】

季康子问:"使民敬、忠以劝，如之何?"子曰:"临之以庄，则敬；孝慈，则忠；举善而教不能，则劝。"

【译文】

季康子问:"要让百姓恭敬，做事尽心尽力并能互相勉励，该怎么办呢?"孔子说:"你行为端正，他们就会对你恭敬；你尊老爱幼，他们就会对你尽心尽力；你选择有能力的人作表率，他们就能互相勉励。"

【English Translation】

Ji Kang Zi enquired of Confucius: "What should one do in order to gain the respect of subordinates, earn their loyalty and cause them to be self motivated?"

Confucius said: "Be mindful of your demeanour and they will be respectful. Be filial and benevolent and they will be faithful. Promote only the good and instruct the unqualified and they will be self-motivated."

How does one win the respect and loyalty of the people? How can they be self-motivated?

An upright official commands respect.

Benevolence and filial piety inspires loyalty.

Employ the efficient and competent.

And the people will be motivated to do their best.

21.

【原文】

或谓孔子曰："子奚不为政?"子曰:"《书》云:'孝乎惟孝,友于兄弟,施于有政',是亦为政,奚其为为政?"

【译文】

有人对孔子说:"你为什么不做官呢?"孔子说:"《尚书》上说:'孝顺父母,友爱兄弟。并让这种风气去影响政治',就是参政了,一定要当官才算参政吗?"

【English Translation】

Someone asked Confucius: "Why do you not join the government?"

Confucius answered: "The *Book of History* says: Be filial to those who deserve it and be loving to one's brothers. This is the essence of government and by promoting this, I'm already involved in governing. Why do you insist governing only means becoming an official?"

22.

【原文】

子曰:"人而无信，不知其可也。大车无輗，小车无軏，其何以行之哉?"

【译文】

孔子说:"一个人不讲信用，怎么可以立身处世。这就好比大车没有套牛的木销子，小车没有套马的木销子，车怎么行驶呢?"

【English Translation】

Confucius said: "How can a person without trustworthiness establish himself? Just as a cart without a collar bar or a carriage without a yoke, how can it be made to move?"

23.

【原文】

子张问：“十世可知也？”子曰：“殷因于夏礼，所损益可知也；周因于殷礼，所损益可知也；其或继周者，虽百世，可知也。”

【译文】

子张问：“我们可以预知十代以后的礼仪制度吗？”孔子说：“殷朝继承夏朝的礼仪制度，其中有废除的和增加的内容，是可以知道的；周朝继承殷朝的礼仪制度其中有废除和增加的内容也是可以知道的。那么，继承周朝的朝代，就是一百代以后的朝代，它的礼仪制度也是可以依此类推而得知的。”

【English Translation】

Zi Zhang enquired: "Is it possible to know the customs and policies practised ten generations later?"

Confucius replied: "Is it possible to know the rites the Yin Dynasty inherited from the Xia Dynasty and the revision that were made? Is it possible to know the customs and practices the Zhou Dynasty inherited from the Yin Dynasty and the revisions they made? Even so with the customs and practices after the Zhou Dynasty, though hundreds of generations may pass, it would be possible to know."

79

24.

【原文】

子曰:"非其鬼而祭之，谄也。
见义不为，无勇也。"

【译文】

孔子说:"不是你该祭的鬼神而去祭，
是谄媚。见到正义而不去伸张，
是没有勇气。"

【English Translation】
Confucius said: "To offer sacrifices to the
dead is merely flattery. Not defending the
righteous is cowardice!"

81

八佾篇第三
Chapter Three, Ba Yi

1.

【原文】

孔子谓季氏："八佾舞于庭，是可忍也，孰不可忍也？"

【译文】

孔子谈到季氏时说："他竟然用天子祭祀时的乐舞，这样违礼的事他都做，还有什么他做不出来呢？"

【English Translation】

Confucius made some comments about Ji Sun Shi saying: "Eight rows of dancers (a dance choreographed exclusively for the king) in his home. If this man is tolerable, who cannot be tolerated? "

2.

【原文】

三家者以《雍》彻。子曰:" 相维辟公,
天子穆穆, 奚取于三家之堂?"

【译文】

孟孙氏, 叔孙氏, 季孙氏三家祭祖时用天子的
礼乐《雍》。孔子说:"天子的礼乐怎能用在大夫的
庙堂上呢?"

【English Translation】

The three families of Lu (namely Meng Sun Shi,
Shu San Shi and Ji Sun Shi) offered sacrifices to their
ancestors by performing the Yong melody.

The 3 families offered sacrifices accompanied by the Yong odes.

The lyrics of the ode say: "attended by the dukes, the king sits solemnly."

HA!

HA!

HA!

They are making a mockery of it since none of these 3 is the son of heaven.

85

3.

【原文】

子曰:"人而不仁, 如礼何?
人而不仁, 如乐何?"

【译文】

孔子说:"做人没有仁爱之心, 还能讲什么礼仪?
做人没有仁爱之心, 还能讲什么音乐?"

【English Translation】

Confucius said: "What is the point of talking about rituals if one does not live a life of love or benevolence? If one does not have love and benevolence, it is futile to talk about music."

One without benevolence.

One without love.

They cannot really perform the rites or appreciate music.

4.

【原文】

林放问礼之本，子曰:"大哉问！礼，与其奢也，宁俭；丧，与其易也，宁戚。"

【译文】

林放问礼的本质是什么，孔子说:"你提的问太大了吧！就一般礼仪来说，与其浪费，不如节俭；就办丧事来说，与其看仪式是否隆重，不如看内心是否悲痛。"

【English Translation】

Ling Fang enquired of Confucius about the essence of customs and Confucius replied saying: "Yours is a big question. Take, for example, common rituals. Is there a need for it to be elaborate? It would be just as well if it is simple. Also, let's take a look at the example of a funeral. Instead of grandeur, sincerity of the heart is more important."

89

5.

【原文】

子曰:"夷狄之有君,
不如诸夏之亡也。"

【译文】

孔子说:"文化落后的国家有君主,
还不如文明国家无国君。对于国家来说,
最重要的不是国君,而是礼仪和文明。"

【English Translation】

Confucius said: "A primitive state of the East
and North might have a monarch but they do not
have any customs. They are worse off than an
advanced state that does not have a
monarch but has a set of well developed customs."

A barbaric tribe with a ruler is worse off ...

... than one which does not have a king but have a set of well developed rites.

Please!

6.

【原文】

季氏旅于泰山。子谓冉有曰："女弗能救与?"
对曰："不能。"子曰："呜呼！曾谓泰山不如林放
乎?"

【译文】

季氏要去祭祀泰山之神。孔子对冉有说："你能
劝阻他吗?"冉有回答说："不能。"孔子说："哎呀！难
道泰山之神还没有鲁国的林放懂礼，竟然会接受季
氏越礼的祭祀?"

【English Translation】

Ji Sun Shi intended to offer sacrifices to the god of
Mount Tai. Confucius questioned Ran You (Confucius'
disciple who works for Ji Shi): "Can you dissuade him
from doing this?"

Ran You replied: "I cannot."

Confucius said: "What an irony? Will the god of
Mount Tai know less about etiquette than Ling Fang
from the state of Lu and accept Ji Sun's offerings?"

Jisun Shi was preparing to offer sacrifices to the god of Mount Tai.

Can you persuade him not to do that?

I can't.

Get out!

Does the god of Mount Tai know less of the rites than Lin Fang and accept Jisun Shi's offerings?

HA! HA!

7.

【原文】

子曰:"君子无所争。必也射乎! 揖让而升,
下而饮。其争也君子。"

【译文】

孔子说:"君子与世无争。如果有争斗一定是射
箭比赛之类的争斗吧! 即使比赛, 也是先谦让再上
场, 射完箭又相互敬酒, 不失其君子风度。"

【English Translation】

Confucius said: "There is no contention between
gentlemen. You may say that there is rivalry in archery.
But even in a competition, one will politely give
precedence to the other. When the competition is over,
each will toast the other and not lose any of the
gentlemen's demeanour."

Among gentlemen, there is no contention except in archery.

At the beginning of the contest, ...

You go first!

At the end of the contest, success is shared.

You're the best!

Cheers!

Even their contention is quite gentlemanly.

95

8.

【原文】

子夏问曰:"'巧笑倩兮, 美目盼兮, 素以为绚兮'。何谓也?"子曰:"绘事后素。"曰:"礼后乎?"子曰:"起予者商也! 始可与言《诗》已矣。"

【译文】

子夏向孔子请教说:"'动人的笑容, 美丽的眼睛, 好像花朵画在洁白的背景上', 这几句诗是什么意思?"孔子说:"绘画要以白色作底。"子夏说:"这个原理是否能说明礼仪要在仁义的基础上才能产生呢?"孔子高兴地说:"你能这样发挥, 现在可以和你谈论《诗经》了。"

【English Translation】

Zi Xia enquired of Confucius: "A captivating smile, beautiful eyes, just like flowers on a white background. What do these verses of the poem mean?"

Confucius replied: "In painting, the subject is always drawn on a white background."

Zi Xia said: "Can I interpret this verse to mean that customs are built on benevolence as a foundation?"

Overjoyed with Zi Xia's insight, Confucius said: "The ability to interpret the verse in this way shows that you are ready to discuss the *Book of Songs* with me."

9.

【原文】

子曰:"夏礼, 吾能言之, 杞不足征也; 殷礼, 吾能言之, 宋不足征也。文献不足故也。足, 则吾能征之矣。"

【译文】

孔子说:"夏朝的礼, 我能讲清楚, 但它的后代杞国我无法引证; 殷朝的礼, 我也能讲清楚, 但它的后代宋国我也无法引证。因为杞国和宋国文献不足的缘故, 如果文献充足, 我就能引证, 可以讲清楚了。"

【English Translation】

Confucius said: "I can expound on the rituals of the Xia and Yin Dynasties but not that of the Qi and Song Dynasties which follow the two former dynasties respectively. This is because there are not enough records about the rituals of these periods. If not, I would be able to explain them too."

10.

【原文】

子曰:"禘自既灌而往者,
吾不欲观之矣。"

【译文】

孔子说:"'禘祭'是属于天子的仪式,
而一个国君用这种仪式,从第一次
献酒以后,我就不想看了。"

【English Translation】

Confucius said: "The ancestral sacrifice ceremony
is only to be performed by the emperor. A king
attempting to execute the ceremony is something
I cannot bear to watch beyond the beginning."

The duke initiated the performance of the Di ceremony.

I cannot bear to watch such violation after the first offering of wine.

Note: The Di ceremony is reserved for the Emperor to perform.

11.

【原文】

或问禘之说，子曰："不知也；知其说者之于天下也，其如示诸斯乎！"指其掌。

【译文】

有人问孔子关于禘祭的理论，孔子说："我不知道。懂得这种理论的人治理起天下来就象翻掌一样容易。"说着指了指自己的手掌。

【English Translation】

Someone enquired of Confucius about ancestral sacrifices.

Confucius replied: "I'm baffled by it too! To the one who knows the answer to this question, governing the world would be a breeze."

12.

【原文】

祭如在，祭神如神在。

子曰："吾不与祭，如不祭。"

【译文】

孔子认为祭祀祖先要像祖先在面前一样，
祭神时就要像神在面前。所以他说："如果
自己不参与祭祀，那和不祭是一样的。"

【English Translation】

Confucius was of the opinion that one must be
earnest when offering sacrifices to ancestors
and behave just as if the ancestors are present.
They must do likewise when offering sacrifices
to the gods. For this reason, it is as good as not
offering any sacrifice if one cannot do it personally.

One should devoutly offer sacrifices to ancestors and the gods as if they were present.

His actions shows his sincerity.

Let me strike the lottery!

In such a situation, it's better not to offer any sacrifices at all.

Not free? I'll burn some incense for you!

105

13.

【原文】

王孙贾问曰:"与其媚于奥, 宁媚于灶, 何谓也?"子曰:"不然。获罪于天, 无所祷也。"

【译文】

王孙贾问孔子:"与其巴结屋角的奥神, 还不如巴结灶神, 说的是什么?"孔子说:"不对, 如果得罪上天, 祈祷谁都没用。"

【English Translation】

Wang Sun enquired of Confucius: "Isn't it better to curry favour Zao (the kitchen god) than to seek the favour of Ao (a god believed to reside in the southern corner of the house believed to rank greater than Zao)?"

Confucius replied: "This is erroneous! When heaven is offended, it is of no use trying to flatter anyone."

107

14.

【原文】

子曰："周监于二代，
郁郁乎文哉！吾从周。"

【译文】

孔子说："周朝借鉴夏、商
两代的礼仪制度建立起周礼，
十分丰富多彩。所以我推崇周礼。"

【English Translation】

Confucius said: "The rites of the Zhou Dynasty
are adapted from a combination of Xia and Yin
Dynasties' rituals. They are full and complete.
Therefore I highly recommend them."

The rites of the Zhou Dynasty are adapted from those of the Xia and Yin Dynasties.

This combination gives them such completeness and diversity. That is why I encourage their use.

15.

【原文】

子入太朝，每事问。或曰："孰谓鄹人之子知礼乎？入太庙，每事问。"子闻之，曰："是礼也。"

【译文】

孔子进入周公庙，碰到不明白的事情就问。有人说："谁说鄹大夫的儿子懂得礼呢？他进入太庙，每件事都问别人。"孔子听说后就说："这就是礼嘛，不懂就问。"

【English Translation】

Confucius entered the temple of Duke Zhou and began asking about all that he did not understand. Someone present began to whisper: "Who says that the son of Mister Zou (Confucius' father) knows the rites and rituals well? When he came into the temple, he had to ask about everything." When Confucius heard this, he said: "To question when one has doubts. Isn't that acting in accordance with the rites?"

Confucius visited the Duke of Zhou's temple.

16.

【原文】
子曰："射不主皮，
为力不同科，古之道也。"

【译文】
孔子说："射箭不一定要射穿箭靶子，
以中不中为输赢，因为各人的力量
不一样，这是古时候的规矩。"

【English Translation】
Confucius said: "When engaging in archery,
it is not necessary to pierce through the target
because the strength of each person varies.
Decide the winner based on the accuracy of
the hit. This is a rule set in the days of old."

Archers are not expected to pierce through the targets with their bows.

Useless cross-bow!

The objective is to hit the target.

113

17.

【原文】

子贡欲去告朔之饩羊。子曰:"赐也! 尔爱其羊, 我爱其礼。"

【译文】

子贡想减免每月初一祭祖时的活羊, 孔子说: "赐啊! 你看重的是羊, 我看重的是礼, 还是不免吧!"

【English Translation】

Zi Gong wanted to do without the sacrificial sheep for the monthly offering to the ancestors. Confucius said to him: "You value the sheep but I value adhering to the rites. It is better not to do without the sheep."

18.

【原文】
子曰:"事君尽礼,
　　人以为谄也。"

【译文】
孔子说:"用臣子的礼去侍奉君主,
　　别人却以为是向君主献媚。"

【English Translation】
Confucius said: "Sigh! The rites of common officials
are employed to serve the prince. Yet the people
think it is the prince's expression of humility."

19.

【原文】

定公问:"君使臣,臣事君,如之何?"孔子
对曰:"君使臣以礼,臣事君以忠。"

【译文】

鲁定公问:"君主使用臣子,臣子服侍君主,应
该是怎样的?"孔子答道:"君主使用臣子应该按照礼
节,臣子侍奉君主应该忠心耿耿。"

【English Translation】

The duke of Ding enquired of Confucius: "How
should a king treat his officials and how should the
officials treat him in return? "

Confucius answered him saying: "A prince should
treat his officials according to the rites and the officials
should give their utmost loyalty in return."

20.

【原文】

子曰:"《关雎》乐而不淫,
哀而不伤。"

【译文】

孔子说:"《关雎》这首诗,
欢快但不放荡, 悲哀却不痛苦。"

【English Translation】
Confucius said: "The poem 'Guan Sui' is
joyful without being insolent, melancholic
but not sorrowful."

21.

【原文】

哀公问社于宰我。宰我对曰:"夏后氏以松,殷人以柏,周人以栗,曰,使民战栗。"子闻之,曰:"成事不说,遂事不谏,既往不咎。"

【译文】

鲁哀公问宰我关于做土地神主应该用什么树木。宰我回答说:"夏朝用松木,商朝用柏木,周朝用栗木,意思是要使百姓战战栗栗。"孔子听了这话后,告诫宰我说:"做过的事不要再提,完成了的事不宜再规劝,已经过去的事不要再责难了。"

【English Translation】

The duke of Ai asked Zai Wo which type of timber is most suitable for sculpting an altar for the guardian spirit of the lands and waters.

Zai Wo answered him saying: "During the Xia Dynasty and Shang Dynasty, pine and cypress were used respectively. But during the Zhou Dynasty, chestnut was used, in order to instil a sense of reverence in the people. (The Chinese character for chestnut was the same character for fear and trembling.)"

When Confucius heard this he said to Zai Wo: "That which has been done should not need to be explained again; that which has its course fixed need not be remonstrated against; that which has passed need not be blamed on anyone."

22.

【原文】

子曰：“管仲之器小哉！”或曰：“管仲俭乎？”曰：“管氏有三归，官事不摄，焉得俭？”“然则管仲知礼乎？”曰：“邦君树塞门，管氏亦树塞门。邦君为两君之好，有反坫，管氏亦有反坫。管氏而知礼，孰不知礼？”

【译文】

孔子说：“管仲的器度狭小啊！”有人问：“管仲节俭吗？”孔子说：“管仲有丰厚的收入，众多的家臣，哪里谈得上节俭呢？”那人又问：“那么管仲是不是很懂礼节？”孔子说：“国君宫里设立照壁，管仲府里也设立照壁；国君为建立外交而设放置酒杯的坫台，管仲府里也有。如果说这样的人也可以叫做懂礼，那世上还有不懂礼的人吗？”

【English Translation】

Confucius said: "Guan Zhong lacks potential."

Someone replied: "He is just being modest."

Confucius said again: "How modest could Guan Zhong who has great wealth and a big family be?"

Someone asked again: "Then can we say that Guan Zhong practises the rites?"

Confucius continued: "The residence of the Guan family is built to rival the palace in beauty and grandeur. If we regard these to be the act of a person who knows the rites, where else can we find someone who doesn't know the rites?"

23.

【原文】

子语鲁大师乐，曰:"乐其可知也: 始作，翕如也; 从之，纯如也，皦如也，绎如也，以成。"

【译文】

孔子告诉鲁国乐师演奏音乐的道理说:"音乐是可以明白的: 开始时合奏; 继而奏出和谐明快的曲调，最后在余音袅袅中结束。"

【English Translation】

Confucius spoke to the musicians of Lu about the principles surrounding performances, saying: "At the onset of the performance, all the instruments should sound together. As the performance develops, the instruments should play in harmony but distinctly. At the end of the performance the sounds should slowly fade to a conclusion. "

Confucius consulted the Grand Musician of Lu about performances.

He asked if performances should start with the whole ensemble playing together, then to have each section playing a distinct melody, and gradually all fade off at the end.

24.

【原文】

仪封人请见，曰:"君子之至于斯也，吾未尝不得见也。"从者见之。出曰:"二三子何患于丧乎？天下之无道也久矣，天将以夫子为木铎。"

【译文】

卫国的边防官请求会见孔子，并说:"凡是有道德学问的人到这里我都要见。"于是，孔子的学生带他去见孔子。他出来后说:"你们这些学生怕什么没官做？天下黑暗的日子已经太久了，上天要让你们的老师给人民带来光明。"

【English Translation】

The chief of border security requested a meeting with Confucius saying: "I've seen all the scholars with morals and knowledge who have been to this place." Hearing this, the disciples of Confucius brought him to see their master. When the chief emerged from a meeting with Confucius he said to Confucius' disciples: "Do not be in a hurry to attain an official post. There is enough darkness in the world. Your teacher will bring light to the people of this world."

129

25.

【原文】

子谓《韶》:"尽美矣,又尽善也。"谓《武》:"尽美矣,未尽善也。"

【译文】

孔子说《韶》乐:"形式好,内容也好。"说《武》乐:"形式好,内容不太好。"

【English Translation】

Confucius praised Shao music saying: "Its form and contents are both good."

But as to Wu music, he said: "Although its form is beautiful, its content leaves a person in want."

Confucius felt that the music of Shao had both good content and form.

As for the music of Wu, it had good form but lacked content.

26.

【原文】

子曰:"居上不宽，为礼不敬，临丧不哀，吾何以观之哉？"

【译文】

孔子说:"职位高却不能宽宏大量，行礼时也不能恭敬严肃，参加丧礼时却不悲哀，这种情形我怎么忍心观看呢？"

【English Translation】

Confucius said: "A person with a high position but lacks magnanimity; a person who is not respectful when bowing; not grieved when attending a funeral -- how can I stand the sight of such a person?"

133

里仁篇第四
Chapter Four, On Virtue

1.

【原文】

子曰:"里仁为美。

择不处仁, 焉得知?"

【译文】

孔子说:"住的地方要选在

风俗淳美的地方,

否则怎么算得上明智呢?"

【English Translation】

Confucius said: "When selecting a place of
residence, one should look for a place
with a good moral climate. If not,
how could one be called wise?"

Choose a place abounding with benevolent people to live in.

Otherwise, how can one be called wise?

2.

【原文】

子曰："不仁者不可以久处约，不可以长处乐。仁者安仁，知者利仁。"

【译文】

孔子说："道德修养差的人做不到安贫乐富。道德修养高的人安于仁，聪明的人利用仁。"

【English Translation】

Confucius said: "Those who have not cultivated morals in themselves will not be able to endure hardship or enjoy prosperity. Those who have a high standard of morality will rest in their virtue and the wise knows the way to gain the benefits of virtue."

I want to be rich.

Those without morals can neither be contented in poverty, ...

I'm happy but ....

... nor health.

Those imbued with morals are content with benevolence.

Take this ...

Thank you.

The wise know what it means to be benevolent.

3.

【原文】

子曰:"唯仁者能好人,
能恶人。"

【译文】

孔子说:"只有道德修养高的人
才能够做到爱憎分明。"

【English Translation】

Confucius said: "Only the virtuous will be able
to see the difference between love and hate."

4.

【原文】
子曰:"苟志于仁矣,
无恶也。"

【译文】
孔子说:"如能立志实行仁德,
就会远离罪恶。"

【English Translation】
Confucius said: "The practice of love
and virtue does not bring harm."

The person who has set his mind on being benevolent.

He is freed from evil.

5.

【原文】

子曰:"富与贵, 是人之所欲也; 不以其道得之, 不处也。贫与贱, 是人之所恶也; 不以其道得之, 不去也。君子去仁, 恶乎成名? 君子无终食之间违仁, 造次必于是, 颠沛必于是。"

【译文】

孔子说:"金钱和地位, 这是人人都想得到的, 如果要用不正当的方法去取得, 宁愿不要。贫穷和下贱, 这是人人都厌恶的, 如果要不用不正当的方法去摆脱, 宁愿不摆脱。君子在任何时候都不违背仁, 匆忙时必定如此。颠沛时必定如此。"

【English Translation】

Confucius said: "Wealth and position are the desires of everyone. But one would rather not have it if to attain it requires the use of unscrupulous means. No one wants to be poor and obscure but the gentleman does not employ dishonest means to escape from it. How can a gentleman who has abandoned morality be known as a gentleman? A gentleman will under no circumstances forget to practise benevolence and morality."

Hey! Want to earn extra pocket money?

Everyone wants to be rich and noble.

Although poor, a gentleman will not acquire wealth and status through unscrupulous means.

A gentleman will not forget to practise benevolence and morality.

143

6.

【原文】

子曰:"我未见好仁者，恶不仁者。好仁者，无以尚之；恶不仁者，其为仁矣，不使不仁者加乎其身。有能一日用其力于仁矣乎？我未见力不足者。盖有之矣，我未之见也。"

【译文】

孔子说:"我没见过爱好仁德的人，也没见过憎恶不仁的人。爱好仁德的人，没什么不好；憎恶不仁的人，他所谓的仁，只不过是怕不仁的人影响自己而已。谁有能力在一天内实行仁德的？这样的人大概是有吧，只是我没有见过。"

【English Translation】

Confucius said: "I have not seen anyone who loves a virtuous and benevolent person. Neither have I seen anyone who hates a person who is not benevolent. There is nothing bad about loving a virtuous and benevolent person. It is only because many are afraid of being influenced negatively that a person who fails to be benevolent is hated. Actually, I have not seen anyone who can achieve virtue and benevolence in a day. But I suppose that there must be one who has done this except that I've not seen him."

I've never seen a man who really loves benevolence,

or truly hates benevolence.

One who truly loves benevolence is virtuous.

NO!

The man who hates benevolence is benevolent because he prevents the malevolent from contaminating him.

Is there one who devotes all his energy to being benevolent?

Surely there must be one although I've never seen him.

145

7.

【原文】

子曰:"人之过也, 各于其党。
观过, 斯知仁矣。"

【译文】

孔子说:"人所犯的错误各有不同,
往往和他们的社会环境、地位有关。
观察一个人的错误, 就可以
知道这个人的社会地位了。"

【English Translation】

Confucius said: "The type of crimes that a
person commits is often related to his social
standing. Therefore by studying the nature of
the mistake, one will know his social status."

8.

【原文】
子曰:"朝闻道,
夕死可矣。"

【译文】
孔子说:"早晨学得真理,
当天晚上死掉也愿意。"

【English Translation】
Confucius said: "If in the morning I
learn of the truth, I shall die without
regrets in the evening."

If one has learnt the truth in the morning, ...

... he will die without regrets in the evening!

I'll sleep in peace tonight!

9.

【原文】

子曰："士志于道，
而耻恶衣恶食者，未足与议也。"

【译文】

孔子说："有志于追求真理，却又以贫困
为耻辱的人，不值得与他讨论真理。"

【English Translation】

Confucius said: "Those who have set their hearts
to pursue the truth, yet take poverty as great
humiliation, are not worth talking to."

151

10.

【原文】

子曰:"君子之于天下也,
无适也,无莫也,义之与比。"

【译文】

孔子说:"天下的事情,并没有固定的模式,
君子只是根据实际情况决定怎样做。"

【English Translation】

Confucius said: "There is no fixed form for all
matters under the sun. A gentleman only acts
according to his assessment of situations."

11.

【原文】

子曰："君子怀德，小人怀土；
君子怀刑，小人怀惠。"

【译文】

孔子说："君子心里装着的是道德，
小人心里装着的是乡土；
君子心里装着的是法纪，
小人心里装着的是私利。"

【English Translation】

Confucius said: "The gentleman yearns for morality while the petty man dreams of home; the gentleman is concerned about laws and legality, the petty man is only worried about personal gains."

A gentleman cherishes virtue.

A petty man cherishes his place of origin.

Papa, I'm hungry!

A gentleman cherishes the law, ...

... but a petty man is preoccupied with self-interest.

12.

【原文】

子曰："放于利而行，多怨。"

【译文】

孔子说："办事从个人利益出发，
多半会招来怨恨。"

【English Translation】
Confucius said: "Carrying out anything
for personal profit will mostly bring about
hatred and bitterness."

157

13.

【原文】

子曰:"能以礼让为国乎，何有？
不能以礼让为国，如礼何？"

【译文】

孔子说:"能用礼让来治理国家，
还会有什么困难呢？
如果不能用礼让来治理国家，
又怎样谈得上实行礼呢？"

【English Translation】

Confucius said: "In state administration, when the
habit of giving in to another is inculcated, what
other problems can arise? If one cannot even
do this, how can one talk about propriety?"

14.

【原文】

子曰："不患无位，患所以立。
不患莫己知，求为可知也？"

【译文】

孔子说："不怕没有职位，
只怕不够条件。不怕别人不知道自己，
只求自己创造出成绩？"

【English Translation】

Confucius said: "Do not be concerned about not
having a position but be concerned about not
having the capacity to fulfil the requirements.
Do not be disturbed by the lack of recognition but be
concerned about the ability to produce good results."

15.

【原文】

子曰:"参乎!吾道一以贯之。"曾子曰:"唯。"子出,门人问曰:"何谓也?"曾子曰:"夫子之道,忠恕而已矣。"

【译文】

孔子说:"参呀!我的学说有一个基本观念贯穿着。"曾子说:"是的。"孔子出门去后,别的学生问曾子:"这是什么意思?"曾子说:"他老人家的学说,只是忠恕罢了。"

【English Translation】

Confucius said:" Oh dear! One of the basic principles of my thesis has been debunked."

Zeng Zi said in response: "Yes, teacher!"

After Confucius had left the house, the other disciples asked Zeng Zi: "What does teacher mean?"

Zeng Zi said: "The teachings of our venerable teacher is merely about loyalty and benevolence."

There is one recurring idea in my doctrine, Zeng.

I agree!

What was the master talking about?

Master Confucius' teachings revolve around loyalty and reciprocity.

16.

【原文】

子曰：“君子喻于义，
　　小人喻于利。”

【译文】

孔子说：“君子明白义的含意，
　　小人懂得利的含意。”

【English Translation】
Confucius said: "A gentleman is well
acquainted with righteousness, the petty
man is acquainted with profit."

164

17.

【原文】

子曰:"见贤思齐焉,
见不贤而内自省也。"

【译文】

孔子说:"遇见德才兼备的人,
就应该向他看齐,遇到无德无才的人,
就应反省自己是不是和他有同样的毛病。"

【English Translation】

Confucius said: "When one meets a person of
substance and high morals, one should look to him
as an example. When one meets a person without
substance or a sense of morality, one should take
him as a foil to examine one's own flaws."

167

18.

【原文】

子曰："事父母几谏。见志不从,
又敬不违, 劳而不怨。"

【译文】

孔子说: "对父母的缺点要委婉地劝说,
父母听不进去, 仍要恭顺他们,
虽心忧而不可怀恨。"

【English Translation】
Confucius said: "One should approach one's
parents with humility when pointing out their
mistakes. When they refuse to heed your
advice, give in to them. Be concerned
but do not harbour bitterness."

19.

【原文】

子曰:"父母在,

不远游, 游必有方。"

【译文】

孔子说:"父母健在,

不轻易出远门, 如必须外出,

一定要告诉父母你的去处。"

【English Translation】

Confucius said: "Avoid leaving home for a
distant journey when one's parents are still alive.
If it is necessary to travel afar, let one's parent
know one's destination."

Avoid going on long journeys when one's parents are alive.

If one has to, one should tell them where one is going.

20.

【原文】

子曰："三年无改于父之道，
可谓孝矣。"

【译文】

孔子说："一个人在父亲去世后三年
之内不改变父亲留下的正确原则，
就可以说他尽孝了。"

【English Translation】

Confucius said: "If a son continues to live by the
principles laid down by his father, three years after
his father's demise, he may be considered filial."

21.

【原文】

子曰:"父母之年,不可不知也。一则以喜,一则以惧。"

【译文】

孔子说:"父母的生日要记挂在心里。一方面为他们长寿而高兴,一方面又为他们老一岁而担忧。"

【English Translation】

Confucius said: "One should always remember the birthdays of one's parents. On the one hand, their longevity is a cause for celebration but on the other hand, their old age is a cause for concern."

Always remember the birthday of one's parents.

Happy Birthday!

It's a happy occasion to celebrate their birthday.

But one is worried to see them grow older.

Worry!

Let's go to the doctor.

175

22.

【原文】

子曰："古者言之不出,

耻躬之不逮也。"

【译文】

孔子说:"古人不轻易说大话,

说得出而做不到,他们会感到羞耻。"

【English Translation】

Confucius said: "The ancients refrained from
boasting. If they failed to live up to their claims,
they will feel utterly disgraced."

In the old days, people were careful with their words.

Lest they failed to live up to it.

23.

【原文】

子曰:"以约失之者鲜矣。"

【译文】

孔子说:"能自律的人
很少犯错误。"

【English Translation】
Confucius said: "Those who are capable of
regulating themselves seldom commit wrong."

A man who is capable of regulating himself.

179

24.

【原文】

子曰："君子欲讷于言
而敏于行。"

【译文】

孔子说:"君子应该说话小心
谨慎, 做事勤劳敏捷。"

【English Translation】

Confucius said: "A gentleman should be
slow to speak but quick to act."

A gentleman is slow to speak ...

... but prompt in action.

25.

【原文】

子曰:"德不孤,

必有邻。"

【译文】

孔子说:"有道德的人是不会孤立的,

一定会有志同道合的人相伴。"

【English Translation】

Confucius said: "A person of morals will
never be lonesome. Others who are like
minded will flock to him."

26.

【原文】

子游曰:"事君数, 斯辱矣;

朋友数, 斯疏矣。"

【译文】

子游说:"对君主频繁进谏, 就会被猜忌;

对朋友劝告太多, 就会被疏远。"

【English Translation】

Zi You said: "To remonstrate excessively before
a king will bring disfavour; excessive rebukes
between friends make a friendship distant."

公冶长篇第五
Chapter 5, Gong Ye Zhang

1.

【原文】

子谓公冶长:"可妻也。虽在缧绁之中，非其罪也。"以其子妻之。

【译文】

孔子谈起公冶长时说:"可以把女儿嫁给他。虽然他曾进过监狱，但不是他的罪过。"把自己的女儿嫁给了公冶长。

【English Translation】

When Confucius talked about Gong Ye Zhang he said: " He would make a good son-in-law. Although he was remanded in prison, it wasn't his fault." After saying this, Confucius gave his daughter's hand in marriage to Gong Ye Zhang.

187

2.

【原文】

子谓南容:"邦有道,不废;邦无道,免于刑戮。"以其兄之子妻之。

【译文】

孔子谈到南容时说:"国家政治清明的时候,他不会被罢官;国家政治黑暗的时候,他也不致遭刑罚。"于是便把自己的侄女嫁给他。

【English Translation】

When Confucius mentioned Nan Rong he said: "If a government is non-corrupt, he would not have been dismissed from the courts. Even if a country is badly run, he would have escaped punishment."

Confucius gave his niece to Nan Rong in marriage.

Nan Rong was an official when the government was honest and efficient.

He was able to hold onto his position without implicating himself when the government was corrupt.

BYE! BYE!

JUST MARRIED

Confucius therefore married his niece to Nan Rong.

3.

【原文】

子谓子贱:"君子哉若人!
鲁无君子者，斯焉取斯?"

【译文】

孔子谈论子贱时说:"君子就是象他这样呀!
如果说鲁国没有君子，他是从哪里
学到这种好品德的呢?"

【English Translation】

Speaking about Lun Zi Jian, Confucius said: "Isn't
this man really a gentleman? If it is true that the
state of Lu does not have any gentleman,
where did he acquire such character from?"

4.

【原文】

子贡问曰："赐也何如？"子曰："女，器也。"
曰："何器也？"曰："瑚琏也。"

【译文】

子贡问孔子："你看我这个人怎么样？"孔子说："你好比器皿。"子贡问："什么器皿？"孔子说："祭祀用的珍品瑚琏。虽然你很有才能，但还不是全才。"

【English Translation】

Zi Gong asked Confucius: "What do you think of me? "

Confucius said: "You are like a vessel."

Zi Gong responded: " What kind of vessel am I?"

Confucius replied: "You are a sacrificial vessel inlaid with gems and precious stone." ("Vessel" is an allusion to a functional object. Comparing Zi Gong to a sacrificial vessel is a complimentary remark, meaning that Zi Gong is capable of great works.)

5.

【原文】

或曰:"雍也仁而不佞。"子曰:"焉用佞? 御人以口给, 屡憎于人。 不知其仁, 焉用佞?"

【译文】

有人说:"冉雍有仁德而不善辩。"孔子说:"何必要善辩呢? 整天与人唇枪舌战地辩驳, 被人讨厌。我不知道他是不是做到了'仁', 但为什么一定要善辩呢?"

【English Translation】

Someone said: "Ran Yong may be benevolent but he lacks oratory skills."

Confucius said: "Of what value is eloquence if it means nitpicking with another all day long and being hated? Whether he is benevolent I do not know. But I see no need for him to be an orator."

195

6.

【原文】

子使漆雕开仕,
对曰:"吾斯之未能信。"子说。

【译文】

孔子叫漆雕开去作官,
漆雕开回答说:"我对这事还没
有完全的把握。"
孔子听了很高兴。

【English Translation】
Confucius persuaded Qi Diao Kai to
become an official. He replied saying: "I'm
not qualified to be an official yet."
Confucius was very glad to hear this.

Confucius advised Qi Diao Kai to take up office.

But I don't trust myself yet.

7.

【原文】

子曰:"道不行, 乘桴浮于海, 从我者, 其由与?"子路闻之喜。子曰:"由也好勇过我, 无所取材。"

【译文】

孔子说:"我的主张不能实行, 我就坐小船去海外, 那时跟随我的人, 大概只有仲由吧!"子路听了这话很高兴。孔子又说:"仲由勇气过人, 却没有什么别长处。"

【English Translation】

Confucius said: "When my schemes did not work out, I travelled to distant places. The only one who remained by my side was Zhong You." Zi You became very happy when he heard this.

Confucius continued: "Zhong You is a man of courage but he lacks any other skill."

199

8.

【原文】

孟武伯问:"子路仁乎?"子曰:"不知也。"又问。子曰:"由也,千乘之国,可使治其赋也,不知其仁也。""求也何如?"子曰:"求也,千室之邑,百乘之家,可使为之宰也,不知其仁也。""赤也何如?"子曰:"赤也,束带立于朝,可使与宾客言也,不知其仁也。"

【译文】

孟武伯问孔子:"子路有仁德吗?"孔子说:"不知道。"孟武伯再次问孔子,孔子说:"仲由呢,可以在一个有千乘兵车的国家里主管军政工作,但不知道他是否有仁德。"孟武伯又问:"冉求这个人怎么样?"孔子回答说:"冉求可以在一个千户人家的县里当县长,或者在大夫封地当总管。有无仁德,我不知道。"孟武伯又问:"公西赤这个人怎么样?"孔子说:"公西赤最适合接待外宾的工作,我也不知道他是否有仁德。"

【English Translation】

Three times Meng Wu Bo persisted in asking Confucius if Zi Lu was benevolent.

Confucius said: "I only know that Zhong You has the ability to command the military force of a country with thousands of troops and chariots. But I do not know if he is benevolent."

Meng Wu Bo asked again: "What about Ran Qiu?"

Confucius replied: "Ran Qiu is capable of being a governor in a city of a thousand families or the chief steward in a senior official's household. But as to whether he is benevolent, I do not know." Meng Wu Bo then directed his attention to Gong Xi Chi and Confucius said: "Gong Xi Chi is best at managing foreign dignitaries when they arrive. But about benevolence, I am not certain if he has such a quality."

9.

【原文】

子谓子贡曰:"女与回也孰愈?"对曰:"赐也何敢望回? 回也闻一以知十, 赐也闻一以知二。"子曰:"弗如也; 吾与女弗如也。"

【译文】

孔子问子贡:"你和颜回谁更强一些?"子贡回答说:"我怎么敢和颜回相比呢, 他学到一个道理可以推知十个道理, 而我学到一个道理却只能推知两个道理。"孔子听后说:"你不如他, 我和你都不如他呀!"

【English Translation】

Confucius asked Zi Gong: "Between you and Yan Hui, who is the greater?"

Yan Hui replied saying: "I wouldn't dare compare myself with him. When he learns of a principle, he is able to deduce ten arguments from it but I can only produce two."

When Confucius heard this he said: "It is true. You cannot be compared with him. Both of us cannot be compared with him."

How would you assess your intellect when compared with Yan Hui?

I daren't compare myself with him!

He can make 10 inference from 1 point.

I can only make two.

I agree with that!

10.

【原文】

宰予昼寝。子曰："朽木不可雕也，粪土之墙不可杇也。于予与何诛？"子曰："始吾于人也，听其言而信其行；今吾于人也，听其言而观其行。于予与改是。"

【译文】

孔子的学生宰予白天睡觉。孔子得知后说："腐朽的木头不能雕刻，粪土的墙壁不能粉刷。对宰予，我责备他做什么？"又说："从前，对于人我是听了他的话就相信了他的行为；现在我是听了他的话还要观察他的行为。是宰予使我改变了对人态度。"

【English Translation】

Confucius' student Zai Yu was found sleeping in the day. Confucius was furious at this and said: "A rotten log cannot be carved with meticulous fine details. A mud wall cannot be painted. Why should I accept responsibility for such a person like Zai Yu?"

Confucius continued: "In the past, I believed everything that a person claimed of himself. But now I will measure a person's words against his actions before I believe his claims. It is Zai Yu who changed my attitude towards people."

Zai Yu was in the habit of taking afternoon naps.

Rotten wood is not suitable to be carved meticulously.

A mud wall cannot be whitewashed. I needn't bother to reproach him.

I used to trust people's words. Now I demand to see their work before trusting them.

It was Zai Yu who changed Confucius' perception of people.

11.

【原文】

子曰:"吾未见刚者。"或对曰:"申枨。"子
曰:"枨也欲, 焉得刚？"

【译文】

孔子说:"我没看见过刚毅的人。"有人说:"申枨
就是。" 孔子说:"申枨有太多欲望, 怎么可能刚
毅？"

【English Translation】

Confucius said: "I have not seen a truly firm and uncompromising person."

Someone suggested: "Isn't Shen Cheng such a person?"

Confucius said: "Shen Cheng is at the mercy of his desires. How can he be considered firm and uncompromising?"

12.

【原文】

子贡曰:"我不欲人之加诸我也,吾亦欲无加诸人。"子曰:"赐也,非尔所及也。"

【译文】

子贡说:"我不想让别人欺侮我,我也不想欺侮别人。"孔子说:"不是你现在可以做到的。"

【English Translation】

Zi Gong said: "I do not do to others what I do not want them to do to me."

Confucius said: "This is not something that you are capable of now."

13.

【原文】

子贡曰:"夫子之文章，可得而闻也；夫子之言性与天道，不可得而闻也。"

【译文】

子贡说:"老师的文献方面的学问，我们有机会听到；老师的人性和天道方面的知识，我们却没有机会听到。"

【English Translation】

Zi Gong said: "I have only heard teacher speak about culture and literature but have never about his views on human nature and the spiritual realm."

Teacher has only covered the subject of ancient literature,

but has hardly spoken about human nature and the way of heaven.

Er....Sorry!

Pay attention!

211

14.

【原文】

子路有闻，未之能行，
唯恐有闻。

【译文】

子路学知识是，已学到的知识
还没有实行就唯恐学新的知识。

【English Translation】
Whenever Zi Lu learned anything new,
he would practise till he mastered it before
proceeding to learn anything new.

213

15.

【原文】

子贡问曰:"孔文子何以谓之'文'也?"子曰:"敏而好学,不耻下问,是以谓之'文'也。"

【译文】

子贡问道:"孔文子因为什么谥为'文'呢?"孔子说:"他聪颖好学,谦虚好问,所以谥称他为'文'。"

【English Translation】

Zi Gong enquired: "Why was Kong Wen given the title Wen (the cultured)?"

Confucius replied: "He was intelligent, keen to learn and humble. That is the reason he was given the title Wen."

Why was Kong Wen Zi called 'cultured'?

It's because he was eager to learn, ...

May I ask you a question?

... and not ashamed to ask those inferior to him in knowledge.

That's why he was known as cultured.

16.

【原文】

子谓子产:"有君子之道四焉: 其行己也恭, 其事上也敬, 其养民也惠, 其使民也义。"

【译文】

孔子评价子产说:"他具有君子的四种美德: 行为端庄, 对君主负责, 对待百姓有恩惠、讲仁义。"

【English Translation】

Kong Zi complimented Zi Chan saying: "He has the four virtues of a king. He carried himself with propriety, showed responsibility to his king, had earned the gratitude of the people and is benevolent to them."

Zi Chang has 4 virtues.

Thanks, I've had enough!

Have another drink!

BAR

He's always courteous.

Good morning.

Humble greetings, Your Majesty.

And reveres his ruler.

Reduce tax!

He is generous to the people.

KEEP IT CLEAN

He shares weal and woe with the commoners.

217

17.

【原文】

子曰：“晏平仲善与人交，
久而敬之。”

【译文】

孔子说：“晏平仲善于与人交朋友，
人们与他交往越久，就越尊敬他。”

【English Translation】

Confucius said: "Yan Ping Zhong is very sociable.
The longer anyone relates with him,
the more that person would respect him."

219

18.

【原文】

子曰："臧文仲居蔡,
山节藻棁，何如其知也？"

【译文】

孔子说："臧文仲 给卜卦用的乌龟建
一间豪华的住所，其实这是违礼的
做法。怎么称得上聪明呢？"

【English Translation】

Confucius said: "Zang Wen Zhong's ingenuity
is merely in providing the divination tortoise
with a luxurious place to live in. Actually,
this is against the rites."

The genius of Zang Wen Zhong is only in giving the ritual tortoise a luxurious mansion.

It's actually against the rites to do that.

19.

【原文】

子张问曰:"令尹子文三仕为令尹，无喜色；三已之，无愠色。旧令尹之政，必以告新令尹。何如?"子曰:"忠矣。"曰:"仁矣乎?"曰:"未知，焉得仁?""崔子弑齐君，陈文子有马十乘，弃而违之，至于他邦，则曰:'犹吾大夫崔子也'.违之。之一邦，则又曰:'犹吾大夫崔子也'.违之。何如?"子曰:"清矣。"曰:"仁矣乎?"曰:"未知，焉得仁?"

【译文】

子张问孔子:"楚国的令尹子文三次担任令尹，不表现出高兴的脸色；三次被免职，亦不露出怨恨的样子。而且每次被免职时都把他做令尹时的政令告诉接任的人。这个人怎么样?"孔子说:"算得上对国家忠心耿耿了。"子张问:"这算不算仁呢?"孔子说:"不知道，这算仁吗?"子张又问:"齐国的大夫崔杼杀了齐庄公，陈文子因此弃官不做，离开了齐国。他到了另一个国家说:'这个国家的执政者跟崔杼是一路货色！'又离开了这个国家到了第三个国家，又说:'这里的执政者跟崔杼也是一路货色'.第三次离开了。你觉得这个人怎么样?"孔子说:"这个人很清高。"子张问:"算得上仁吗?"孔子说:"不知道，这算仁吗?"

【English Translation】

Zi Zhang asked Confucius: "Wen of the state of Chu, was appointed prefect three times, but each time, he did not express any joy on his face. Three times he was demoted, but he neither showed any anger or bitterness. In addition, every time he had to leave the position, he never failed to explain the duties of the appointment to his successor. How would you assess such a person?"

Confucius said: "I don't know. Can this be considered as benevolence?"

Zi Zhang asked again: "When Officer Cui of the state of Qi murdered his king, Xuan Gong, Wen resigned from his post there and left Qi. After travelling to another country, he said 'The rulers of this place is just like Cui.' and then left for yet another country. What do you think of him?"

Confucius replied: "This is a person of impeccable morals."

Zi Zhang asked: "Is he benevolent?"

Confucius replied: "I don't know. How can this show whether he is benevolent?"

He responsibly told his successors how to carry on with the policies he had implemented.

Zi Wen kept a straight face when appointed to and removed from office.

No, it's only loyalty.

Is this benevolence?

Traitor.

When Duke Zhuang was assassinated, Chen Wen Zi of Qi gave up his post because of the evil done.

He left his new position twice as the rulers in these other 2 states are just as evil as Cui Zi.

I still cannot call him "benevolent" but perhaps just "pure".

20.

【原文】

季文子三思而后行。子闻之,
曰:"再, 斯可矣。"

【译文】

季文子办事要考虑再三才实行。
孔子听后说:"遇事考虑两次就可以了。"

【English Translation】

Everything that Ji Wen Zi did, he would
consider the matter thrice before acting.
After hearing this Confucius said:
"Twice would have been enough."

21.

【原文】

子曰:"宁武子, 邦有道, 则知; 邦无道, 则愚。其知可及也, 其愚不可及也。"

【译文】

孔子说:"宁武子这个人, 国家政治清明的时候, 他就聪明; 国家政治黑暗的时候, 便装糊涂。他的聪明, 别人可以做到; 他的'糊涂', 别人就做不到。"

【English Translation】

Confucius said: "Ning Wu Zi demonstrates his intelligence when the king runs a just and effective government. When the king is corrupt and the government is anarchic, Ning Wu Zi acts like a stupid man. One can match his intelligence but not match his folly."

Ning Wu Zi was intelligent when the government was enlightened.

Anyone can match his intelligence.

Ha! Ha! Sorry!

All wrong, Sir!

But no one can match his stupidity.

But when the government was weak, he made mistakes.

22.

【原文】

子在陈，曰："归与！归与！吾党之小子狂简，斐然成章，不知所以裁之。"

【译文】

孔子出游陈国，一再对随行的学生说："回去吧！回去吧！我家里的学生都是有远大抱负，又文采斐然的，只是不知道怎样节制自己。"

【English Translation】

Confucius was travelling in the state of Chen. He repeatedly told his students: "Let's return home! Let's return home!' The other students of mine have lofty ambitions and great potential. However they lack restraint."

When Confucius was in the state of Chen, he constantly thought of his disciples.

He said: My students have lofty ambitions and great potential, but are unable to regulate themselves.

23.

【原文】

子曰："伯夷、叔齐不念旧恶，
怨是用希。"

【译文】

孔子说："伯夷，叔齐两兄弟不记
过去的仇恨，遗留的怨恨也少。"

【English Translation】

Confucius said: "Bo Yi and Shu Qi never harboured
any grudges against anyone. There are very few
who have any misgivings about them."

The brothers, Bo Yi and Shu Qi, did not bear grudges.

Those stupid fellows sold their home.

That was why they incurred little ill will.

24.

【原文】

子曰:"孰谓微生高直? 或乞醯焉,
乞诸其邻而与之。"

【译文】

孔子说:"谁说微生高直爽? 有人向他
借点醋, 他向邻居借来再转借给那人
却不肯说自己没有。"

【English Translation】

Confucius said: "Does anyone think Wei Sheng
is really noble and generous? When someone
sought to borrow some vinegar from him, he
went to his neighbour to borrow some so as
to lend it away but refused to admit it."

233

25.

【原文】

子曰："巧言、令色、足恭，左丘明耻之，丘亦耻之。匿怨而友其人，左丘明耻之，丘亦耻之。"

【译文】

孔子说："花言巧语，伪装和善，过分谦恭，左丘明认为是可耻的，我也认为是可耻的。藏匿对一个人的怨恨而装出友好的样子，左丘明认为是可耻的，我也认为是可耻的。"

【English Translation】

Confucius said: "A glib tongue, false affability, exaggerated humility and hatred concealed with a false front of friendliness. Zhuo Qiu Ming regards these as shameful behaviour and so do I."

Both Confucius and Zuo Qing Ming dislike flattery and wheedling.

Great looking suit, Sir!

I'm being ignored!

I'll get back at him one day.

To hide enmity with a false front, Zuo Qing Ming despised,

And so do I.

26.

【原文】

颜渊、季路侍。子曰:"盍各言尔志?"子路曰:"愿车马衣裘与朋友共, 敝之而无憾。"颜渊曰:"愿无伐善, 无施劳。"子路曰:"愿闻子之志。"子曰:"老者安之, 朋友信之, 少者怀之。"

【译文】

有一次颜回, 季路在老师身边听讲。孔子说:"说说你们各自的志向好吗?"子路说:"我愿意把车马衣服同朋友共享, 用坏了也不觉得遗憾。"颜回说:"我想做到不夸耀自己的长处, 不表白自己的功劳。"子路对孔子说:"想听您的志向。"孔子说:"我愿老年人平安, 朋友们互相信任, 少年人得到关怀。"

【English Translation】

Once, when Yan Hui and Li Lu was sitting at the feet of Confucius to listen to him, Confucius said: "Tell me about your ambitions."

Zi Lu said: "I wish to be able to share my horses, carriage and clothes with my friends. Even if they spoil these things I will not get angry."

Yan Hui said: "My only hope is that I will not boast of my virtues nor claim credits for the favours I do for others."

Zi Lu turned to Confucius and said: "We would like to hear about teacher's wish."

Confucius replied saying: "For the aged, I hope to be of comfort; toward friends, to be of good faith. In dealing with the young, to cherish them."

27.

【原文】

子曰:"已矣乎！吾未见能见
其过而内自讼者也。"

【译文】

孔子说:"算了吧！我没有见到过能
发现自己的过错而从内心深处
进行自我批判的人。"

【English Translation】
Confucius said: "Forget it! I've not seen
anyone who could criticize his own faults."

There are many kinds of people around.

OH! NO!

But I've not seen anyone who is able to discern his errors.

28.

【原文】

子曰:"十室之邑，必有忠信如丘者焉，不如丘之好学也。"

【译文】

孔子说:"有人家的地方，一定都有像我这样忠诚和讲信用的人，只是不如我爱好学习罢了。"

【English Translation】

Confucius said: "Wherever humans live, there will be someone who is as loyal and trustworthy as I am. The only difference between them and me is my love for learning."

But few are as eager to learn as Confucius.

雍也篇第六
Chapter Six, About Yong Ye

1.

【原文】

子曰:"雍也可使南面。"

【译文】

孔子说:"冉雍
是可以做大官的。"

【English Translation】

Confucius said: "Ran You has the
potential to become a high official."

Confucius said that Ran Yong was ministerial material.

243

2.

【原文】

仲弓问子桑伯子，子曰："可也简。"仲弓曰："居敬而行简，以临其民，不亦可乎？居简而行简，无乃大简乎？"子曰："雍之言然。"

【译文】

冉雍问子桑伯子这人怎么样，孔子说："为人还可以，办事很简约。"冉雍说："立身庄重又办事简约，这样来治理百姓不是好办法吗？如果立身简约而办事简约，那不是不负责吗？"孔子说："你的话很有道理。"

【English Translation】

Ran You asked Zi Sang what Bo Zi was like.

Confucius replied: "He is reasonable and handles matters simply and efficiently."

Ran You said: "If one is serious about work and focused on the important matters, will that not make him a good administrator of the people? If a person only pays attention to important matters and is lax in his own conduct, isn't that being irresponsible?"

Confucius replied: "You are right!"

3.

【原文】

哀公问:"弟子孰为好学?"孔子对曰:"有颜回者好学,不迁怒,不贰过。不幸短命死矣。今也则亡,未闻好学者也。"

【译文】

鲁哀公问孔子:"你的学生中谁最爱学习?"孔子回答说:"有一个叫颜回的最爱学习,不对人发脾气,知错能改。不幸短命死了。现在没有了,没有听说有爱学习的人了。"

【English Translation】

Duke Ai of Lu asked Confucius: "Of all your students, who is the one who loves learning the most?"

Confucius replied: "A student of mine named Yan Hui was the keenest to learn, was polite and accepted rebuke readily. Unfortunately he lived a short life. There is no one with as much desire to learn as Yan Hui now."

4.

【原文】

子华使于齐，冉子为其母请粟，子曰："与之釜。"请益，曰："与之庾。"冉子与之粟五秉。子曰："赤之适齐也，乘肥马，衣轻裘。吾闻之也：君子周急不继富。"

【译文】

公西华被派往齐国去作使者，冉有为公西华的母亲请求谷子补贴，孔子说："给他六斗四升。"冉有请求多给一些，孔子说："再给她二斗四升。"冉有却给了她八十石。孔子说："公西华到齐国去，乘坐肥壮的马拉的车子，穿着轻暖的皮袍。我听说过：君子救济急难而不是增加别人的财富。"

【English Translation】

Gong Xi Hua was sent to the state of Qi to be an envoy. Ran You came to Confucius on behalf of Gong Xi Hua's mother to ask for some grain.

Confucius ordered: "Let him have two *dou* and four *shen* of grain."

But Ran You requested Confucius to be more generous. So Confucius said: "Let him have two *dou* and four *shen* more grain."

But Ran You asked for even more. He suggested that Confucius gave Gong Xi Hua's mother eighty stones worth of grain."

Annoyed to hear this Confucius said: "Gong Xi Hua has gone to the state of Qi on a carriage drawn by well fed horses, and clad in fur.

249

5.

【原文】

原思为之宰，与之粟九百，辞。子曰：
"毋！以与尔邻里乡党乎！"

【译文】

原思做孔家的总管，孔子给他九百斗谷子，原
思推辞不受。孔子说："不要推辞，你可以把谷子给
家乡的穷人嘛。"

【English Translation】

Yuan Si was the chief housekeeper of Confucius.
Confucius gave him nine hundred *dou* of grain but he
refused to accept it.

Confucius said: "Please do not reject my gift. You
could give the grain to those who in your village do not
have enough."

Confucius wanted to give Yuan Si some grain.

6.

【原文】

子谓仲弓，曰："犁牛之子骍且角，虽欲勿用，山川其舍诸？"

【译文】

孔子谈论冉雍时说："小耕牛毛角红润，双角端正。虽耕牛不可用来祭祀，但山川之神会舍弃它吗？冉雍就象小耕牛，出身虽然贫贱，但他也有作官的才能。"

【English Translation】

When Confucius was talking about Ran You he said: "Although Ran You was poor he has great potential to become an official."

Such a sturdy calf shouldn't be used as a sacrifice.

Confucius likened Ran Yong to a calf.

The gods of the mountains and rivers will not reject his service.

How fitting!

Thank you.

Great job!

7.

【原文】

子曰："回也，其心三月不违仁，其余则日月至焉而已矣。"

【译文】

孔子说："颜回啊，他的心里可以长期不违背仁德，至于其余的学生只不过有时想一下仁德。"

【English Translation】

Confucius said: "Only Yan Hui can practise benevolence constantly while the other students only think about it occasionally."

Yan Hui constantly had benevolence on his mind.

Unlike the other disciples who only thought about it occasionally.

8.

【原文】

季康子问:"仲由可使从政也与?"子曰:"由也果,于从政乎何有?"曰:"赐也可使从政也与?"曰:"赐也达,于从政乎何有?"曰:"求也可使从政也与?"曰:"求也艺,与从政乎何有?"

【译文】

季康子问孔子:"仲由可以作官么?"孔子说:"仲由遇事果断,有什么不可以作官的呢?"季康子又问:"端木赐可以作官么?"孔子说:"端木赐通达人情事理,有什么不可以作官的呢?"季康子又问:"冉求可以作官么?"孔子说:"冉求多才多艺,有什么不可以作官的呢?"

【English Translation】

Ji Kang Zi asked Confucius: "Can Zhong You become an official?"

Confucius replied: "Zhong You is quick and decisive when he works. Would it be difficult for someone like him to become an official?"

Ji Kang Zi continued to ask Confucius: "Can Duanmu Ci become an official?"

Confucius answered him, saying: "Duanmu Ci understands human relationships very well. What difficulty would he encounter if he enters the court's service?"

Ji Kang Zi then continued to ask : "Can Ran Qiu take up office as a court official?"

Confucius replied: "Ran Qiu is a man of many talents. Becoming an official is no difficulty to him."

Can Zhong You be an official?

With Zhong You's tenacity, what difficulty can he encounter?

I'm very confident it's a fact.

Can Duanmu Ci be an official?

With his understanding of human relations, what difficulty can he encounter?

Take it easy.

Can Ran Qiu be an official?

With Ran Qiu's versatility, what problems can he encounter?

9.

【原文】

季氏使闵子骞为费宰。闵子骞曰:"善为我辞焉!如有复我者,则吾必在汶上矣。"

【译文】

季氏派人请闵子骞做费邑县长。闵子骞对来人说:"请回去美言几句帮我辞掉吧!如果再派人来召我,那我一定躲到汶水那边的齐国去了。"

【English Translation】

The Ji family invited Min Zi Qian to take the governor's seat in the Pi prefecture. Min Zi Qian said to the messenger: "Please return to your master and politely refuse the position on my behalf. If anyone is sent to persuade me again, I will flee to the state of Qi near river Wen."

Note: Min Zi Qian refused to accept the appointment because he refused to be in cahoots with the disloyal Lord Ji Shun.

10.

【原文】

伯牛有疾，子问之，自牖执其手，曰："亡之，命矣夫！斯人也而有斯疾也！斯人也而有斯疾也！"

【译文】

伯牛得了重病，孔子去探望他，从窗口拉着他的手劝慰着说："生死有命呀！这样的人竟得了这样的病！这样的人竟得了这样的病！"

【English Translation】

Bo Niu was ill. Confucius paid him a visit and holding his hand comforted him: "Life and death are decreed by heaven. Oh, I never thought someone like you would be stricken by such sickness."

261

11.

【原文】

子曰："贤哉，回也！一箪食，一瓢饮，在陋巷，人不堪其忧，回也不改其乐。贤哉！回也！"

【译文】

孔子说："修养多好啊，颜回呀！粗茶淡饭，住在简陋的巷子里，别人都受不了那种困苦，而他却依然快快乐乐。修养多好啊，颜回呀！"

【English Translation】

Confucius said: "Yan Hui is a cultured person, he is content with simple food and plain water and lives in a crumbling house in a narrow lane. Everyone else cannot withstand such harsh conditions but he even managed to live happily without allowing himself to be swayed from his resolutions. How admirable is Yan Hui's virtue."

Yan Hui is very gracious and cultured.

Instant noodles

He lives on simple fare.

And plain water.

He lives in a dilapidated house; a lifestyle others cannot endure.

But manages to remain bright and cheerful.

Only Yan Hui has such refinement.

263

12.

【原文】

冉求曰:"非不说子之道，力不足也。"子曰:"力不足者，中道而废，今女画。"

【译文】

冉求说:"老师，不是我不喜欢您的学说，是我的领悟能力不够。"孔子说:"如果真是能力不够，走到半道就会再也走不动了，而你还没有起步就说走不动了。"

【English Translation】

Ran Qiu said to the teacher: "It is not that I do not like your teachings, but just that it demands too much from me."

Confucius responded: "If what you say is true, it would be like a man who has travelled a distance on a long journey and found that he is not able to complete the course. But as for you, you have not even taken your first step."

13.

【原文】

子谓子夏曰:"女为君子儒,
无为小人儒。"

【译文】

孔子对子夏说:"你要做一个
道德高尚的儒生,
不要做道德低下的儒生。"

【English Translation】

Confucius said to Zi Xia: "You must aspire to be a scholar of the highest morals and integrity; not a licentious and dishonest scholar."

14.

【原文】

子游为武城宰。子曰:"女得人焉耳乎?"
曰:"有澹台灭明者,行不由径,非公事,未尝
至于偃之室也。"

【译文】

子游做鲁国武城县长的时候,孔子问他:"你得
到什么人才了吗?"子游回答说:"有一个叫澹台灭明
的人,不走邪道,不是为公事就不会来我家求助。"

【English Translation】

When Zi You was the governor of Wu Cheng,
Confucius asked him: "Have you discovered any
capable men?"

Zi You replied saying: "I have found one Dantai
Mieming who never used unscrupulous ways and never
bothers me unless it pertains to matters of work."

269

15.

【原文】

子曰:"孟之反不伐, 奔而殿, 将入门, 策其马, 曰: '非敢后也, 马不进也。'"

【译文】

孔子说:"有一次孟之反和齐国打仗败退下来, 他走在最后, 掩护全军, 将入城门时, 用鞭子打着马说: '不是我敢于殿后, 是这匹马跑不快。'"

【English Translation】

Confucius says: "Once when Meng Zhi Fan's troops was retreating from a battle against the Qi army, he trailed his troops in order to cover their rear. When he finally entered into the fortress, he whipped his horse saying: 'It is not that I do not want to ride faster but this horse simply would not run.' "

16.

【原文】

子曰："不有祝鮀之佞，而有宋朝之美，难乎免于今之世矣。"

【译文】

孔子说："如果没有祝鮀的善辩口才，仅有公子朝的美貌，在当今的社会里怕是祸害难免了。"

【English Translation】

Confucius said: "Without the eloquence of Tuo and the beauty of Prince Chao of the Song Dynasty it is difficult to escape the perils of the present age."

(Note: Prince Chao is known for seductiveness and his incestuous relationship with half sister Nan-Zi.)

We must be understanding toward the vertically challenged.

It's difficult to avoid the perils of the present age without the eloquence of Zhao.

And the charm of Prince Zhao of Song.

17.

【原文】

子曰："谁能出不由户？

何莫由斯道也？"

【译文】

孔子说："有谁能够出门时不经过门口呢？

为什么就没有人经过仁义这条路呢？"

【English Translation】

Confucius said: "Who can leave the house without

passing through the door? Why is it that no one

would walk through our door of benevolence?"

No one can leave a house except through the door.

Note: Confucius uses this analogy to illustrate that it is second nature for humans to be benevolent.

18.

【原文】

子曰:"质胜文则野，文胜质则史。文质彬彬，然后君子。"

【译文】

孔子说:"一个人质朴多于文彩，就会显得粗俗，如果文彩多于质朴，就会显得虚浮，文彩和质朴配合适当，才是君子风度。"

【English Translation】

Confucius says: "The person who lives more of a life of austerity than erudition will appear brutish. If a person is more erudite than austere, it would make him seem pretentious. Only with the right mix of erudition and austerity can he be considered gentlemanly."

19.

【原文】

子曰："人之生也直,

罔之生也幸而免。"

【译文】

孔子说:"人的生存之道在于正直,

不正直的人也能生存, 那是侥幸。"

【English Translation】

Confucius said: "A person's survival depends

on his integrity. Those who lack integrity

only survive by a stroke of luck."

20.

【原文】

子曰："知之者不如好之者，
好之者不如乐之者。"

【译文】

孔子说："懂得学业的人不如喜爱学业的人，
喜爱学业的人不如以学业为乐的人。"

【English Translation】

Confucius said: "Those who have knowledge
cannot be compared with those who love knowledge.
But even those who love knowledge cannot compare
with those who delight in knowledge."

21.

【原文】

子曰:"中人以上, 可以语上也; 中人以下, 不可以语上也。"

【译文】

孔子说:"接受能力在中等以上的人, 可以给他们传授高深的知识; 接受能力在中等以下的人, 不可以对他们传授高深的知识。"

【English Translation】

Confucius said: "To those above average, higher knowledge may be transmitted to them. To those who are below average, higher knowledge cannot be transmitted."

Those who are above average intellectually can have advanced knowledge transmitted to them.

But advanced knowledge cannot be transmitted to those who are intellectually below average.

22.

【原文】

樊迟问知，子曰："务民之义，敬鬼神而远之，可谓知矣。"问仁，曰："仁者先难而后获，可谓仁矣。"

【译文】

樊迟问怎样才算明智，孔子说："善于劝导人民重义，对鬼神敬而远之，可以算是明智了。"樊迟又问怎样才算有仁德，孔子说："有仁德的人艰难的工作走在前面，论功行赏时落于人后，这可以叫有仁德了。"

【English Translation】

Fan Chi asked about wisdom. Confucius answered saying: "One may be deemed wise if one will convince the people to be loyal, and to be reverent to the gods and spirits."

Fan Chi continued to ask: "What is benevolence?"

Confucius said: "Benevolence involves being the first to volunteer for a difficult job and the last to think about rewards and recognition."

285

23.

【原文】

子曰："知者乐水，仁者乐山。知者动，仁者静。知者乐，仁者寿。"

【译文】

孔子说："聪明的人喜爱水，有仁德的人喜爱山。聪明的人好动，有仁德的人好静。聪明的人生活快乐，有仁德的人长寿。"

【English Translation】

Confucius says: "The wise delights in flowing waters and the benevolent delights in the hills. The wise are active, the benevolent are reticent. The wise lives a happy life and the benevolent achieves longevity."

The wise delights in water.

The benevolent delights in the mountains.

The wise is active.

The benevolent is at rest.

The wise enjoys life.

While the benevolent achieves longevity.

287

24.

【原文】

子曰:"齐一变, 至于鲁;
鲁一变, 至于道。"

【译文】

孔子说:"如果齐国变革,
可以达到鲁国现在的水平;
如果鲁国变革,
便进而合于大道了。"

【English Translation】

Confucius says: "If the state of Qi makes reforms,
it can reach the level of the state of Lu. If the state
of Lu makes reforms, it will be travelling on the
road towards benevolence."

289

25.

【原文】

子曰:"觚不觚,

觚哉! 觚哉!"

【译文】

孔子感叹说:"现在觚这种礼器不像

觚的样子,还能算是觚吗!"

【English Translation】

Confucius sighed: "The Gu we have today hardly

looks like a Gu. How can it be called a Gu?"

NB: Gu refers to a sacrificial vessel for holding wine.

Confucius lamented:"The Gu these days is hardly like the ancient Gu."

Eh?

Note: Gu is a sacrificial vessel.

26.

【原文】

宰我问曰:"仁者, 虽告之曰, '井有仁焉', 其从之也?"子曰:"何为其然也? 君子可逝也, 不可陷也; 可欺也, 不可罔也。"

【译文】

宰我问道:"有仁德的人, 就是告诉他: '井底有人!' 他会跳下去吗?"孔子说:"你怎么能这样提问题呢? 君子会去救人, 却不会自己也跳下去; 可能被欺骗, 却不可以受愚弄。"

【English Translation】

Zai Wo asked: "If a person is benevolent, by telling him that someone has fallen into a well, will it cause him to jump in after the victim to attempt a rescue? "

Confucius said: "How can you raise such a question? A gentleman may give up his life but will not jump into the well. Although he may be deceived, he will not commit a foolish act."

27.

【原文】

子曰："君子博学于文，

约之以礼，

亦可以弗畔矣夫！"

【译文】

孔子说："君子广泛地学习文化，

并用礼来约束自己，

就可避免离经叛道了。"

【English Translation】

Confucius said: "The gentleman devotes himself
to the learning of culture so that he can use the
rites to restrain himself. This will keep him
from doing any wrong."

A man who diligently studies and regulates himself with the rites.

No!

He cannot go astray.

Well done!

Lucky!

28.

【原文】

子见南子，子路不说。夫子矢之曰："予所否者，天厌之！天厌之！"

【译文】

孔子去见名声不好的卫灵公夫人南子，子路很不高兴。孔子发誓说："我如果做了不正当的事，天理也不容！天理也不容!"

【English Translation】

Confucius' visit to the queen consort Nan Zi raised the ire of Zi Lu. Confucius said: "If I behaved indecently, heaven will not condone my acts! Heaven will not condone!"

297

29.

【原文】

子曰："中庸之为德也,

其至矣乎!

民鲜久矣。"

【译文】

孔子说:"中庸作为一种道德,

已达到最高境界了!可是

人们已经很久不提它了。"

【English Translation】

Confucius said: "The Doctrine of the Constant

Mean is the perfect virtue but it is seldom

mentioned these days."

30.

【原文】

子贡曰:"如有博施于民而能济众,何如? 可谓仁乎?"子曰:"何事于仁! 必也圣乎! 尧舜其犹病诸! 夫仁者, 己欲立而立人, 己欲达而达人。能近取譬, 可谓仁之方也已。"

【译文】

子贡问孔子:"如果有人能广泛地给人民带来好处, 使大家生活富裕, 这个人可算得上仁人吗?"孔子说:"岂止是仁人, 一定是圣人了! 只怕是上尧, 帝舜也做不到这样呢! 所谓仁人就是自己想树立的也帮别人树立, 自己想达到的也帮别人达到。能够凡事想到自己就推及别人, 这就是仁人的处世态度。"

【English Translation】

Zi Gong asked Confucius: "If a person brings benefits to his community, and causes everyone to prosper, is this person considered benevolent?"

Confucius replied: "This would be more than a benevolent person. He would be a saint who is even unmatched by Yao and Shun. A benevolent person is one who would assist others to establish what he wants to establish; assist others to achieve what he wants to achieve. Always keep in mind mutual benefits as the hallmark of a benevolent person."

述而篇第七
Chapter 7, On Transmitting

1.

【原文】
子曰:"述而不作,
信而好古,
窃比于我老彭。"

【译文】
孔子说:"阐述古籍而不随意创作,
相信并爱好古代文化,
我自认为可以与老子和彭祖相比了。"

【English Translation】
Confucius said: "I expound the ancient texts but have not flippantly created new works, and thus consider myself on the same level as Peng Zu."

Confucius adapted and did not frivolously create because he loved ancient culture.

Privately, I compare myself with Old Peng.

2.

【原文】

子曰:"默而识之,

学而不厌, 诲人不倦,

何有于我哉?"

【译文】

孔子说:"对于知识博闻强记,

学习努力而不满足,

教导别人不知疲倦,

这些事情我做到了吗?"

【English Translation】

Confucius said: "To remember all that I've seen
or heard, never to be contented with my learning
and never to tire of teaching others. These are
the merit I can confidently claim."

3.

【原文】

子曰:"德之不修，学之不讲，
闻义不能徙，不善不能改，
是吾忧也。"

【译文】

孔子说:"不培养品德，不讲习学问，
见到正义的事不能去做，
有缺点不能改正，
这些都是我所忧虑的事。"

【English Translation】

Confucius said: "Not cultivating virtue, not
perfecting my learning, not practising righteousness,
rectifying my shortcomings: these are things
that I worry about most."

Not improving morally.

Another glass won't hurt!

Not practising what one has learnt.

Not being able to uphold righteousness personally. Not being able to change what is not good.

I'm worried about these.

4.

【原文】

子之燕居,

申申如也, 天天如也。

【译文】

孔子在家闲住的时候,

衣着整齐, 心情舒畅。

【English Translation】

When Confucius was at home, he always made
himself look neat, and was relaxed and cheerful.

5.

【原文】

子曰:"甚矣, 吾衰也!
久矣, 吾不复梦见周公!"

【译文】

孔子说:"唉!我老了, 已经
很长时间没有再梦见周公了。"

【English Translation】
Confucius said: "Oh! I must be getting old. It's
been a long time since I saw the Duke of Zhou."

NB: The Duke of Zhou was one of Confucius'
most venerated sages. He was the founder of Lu
and the ritual system in the state.

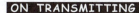

6.

【原文】

子曰:"志于道, 据于德,
依于仁, 游于艺。"

【译文】

孔子说:"以道为志向,
以德为基础, 以仁为依靠, 游习于六艺
（礼仪, 音乐, 射技, 驾车, 文字, 算术）之中。"

【English Translation】

Confucius said: "Set you heart on the way, support
yourself by its virtue, lean upon benevolence and
seek amusement in the arts. (The six arts refer to
rites, music, archery, carriage driving,
literature and mathematics). "

Note: To Confucius, a scholar should possess six skills: namely, music, rites, archery, carriage driving, arithmetic and literature.

7.

【原文】

子曰:"自行束修以上,
吾未尝无诲焉。"

【译文】

孔子说:"凡十五岁以上的成童来学习,
我没有不教诲的。"

【English Translation】

Confucius said: "Whenever anyone wearing a Shu
Xiu came to learn from me, I never rejected him."

NB: Shu Xiu refers to a head cloth worn by
adolescents when they are about fifteen.

8.

【原文】

子曰:"不愤不启,不悱不发。举一隅不以三隅反,则不复也。"

【译文】

孔子说:"我教导学生,不到他们苦苦思索也不能明白的时候,不去开导他们;不到他们想说又不知道怎么说的时候,不去启发他们;我教给他们某种知识,如果他们不能举一反三,我就不再教他们了。"

【English Translation】

Confucius said: "Not until my students have struggled to no avail with their doubts and questions will I intervene to guide them along. If for every principle that I propose, they do not derive three other observations, I will stop teaching them."

I can't figure this out.

Confucius only helped his students after they have tried hard.

What can you conclude from these?

If his students could not draw inferences from his teachings, ...

... he would not repeat himself.

I think I understand.

9.

【原文】
子食于有丧者之侧，
未赏饱过。

【译文】
孔子和死了亲属的人一起吃饭，
不曾吃饱过。

【English Translation】
Confucius never had his fill of a meal whenever
he sat beside someone who was bereaved.

10.

【原文】
子于是日哭,
则不歌。

【译文】
孔子在吊丧哭泣过的那
一天, 就不再唱歌。

【English Translation】
Confucius would never sing for the whole
day whenever he attended a funeral.

11.

【原文】

子谓颜渊曰:"用之则行, 舍之则藏, 惟我与尔有是夫!"子路曰:"子行三军, 则谁与?"子曰:"暴虎冯河, 死而无悔者, 吾不与也。必也临事而惧, 好谋而成者也。"

【译文】

孔子对颜渊说:"国君用我, 我就出面做事, 不用我, 我就不露面, 能做到这样的只有我和你吧!"子路问道:"您若指挥军队, 愿意找谁共事?"孔子说:"赤手空拳敢打老虎, 徒步敢过大河, 死了也不后悔的人, 我是不会和他共事的。同我共事的人应该是遇事谨慎小心, 善于思考并能完成任务的人。"

【English Translation】

Confucius said to Yan Yuan: "If the emperor took me into his service, I would come to the forefront to represent him. If he chooses not to employ my services, I would withdraw from the limelight unperturbed. Only you and I are capable of this. "

Zi Lu asked: "Who would you appoint to direct the army?"

Confucius said: "I will not collaborate with anyone who attempts to attack a tiger with bare hands or crosses a river without considering its depth and takes lightly his own life. Anyone who works with me should be careful in all he does. He would contemplate the consequence of an action before carrying it out."

323

12.

【原文】

子曰:"富而可求也,虽执鞭之士,吾亦为之。如不可求,从吾所好。"

【译文】

孔子说:"财富如果来路正当,就是替人执鞭的下等差事我也干。如果财富来路不正,我还是做我自己爱好的事情。"

【English Translation】

Confucius said: "If the means by which wealth is acquired is legitimate, even if it means being a common cart driver, I would do it willingly. If it is obtained illegitimately, then I would be inclined to pursue the things that I love."

Confucius said he did not mind being a cart driver because he would only become rich through legitimate means.

If wealth could not be obtained legitimately, I'd rather do what I like.

Today's Lesson

13.

【原文】
子之所慎：
斋，战，疾。

【译文】
孔子谈起来最为谨慎的三件事是：
斋戒、战争、疾病。

【English Translation】
Speaking about the things which Confucius is
most cautious of, he said: "They are fasting,
war and disease."

Confucius paid the most
attention to fasting, ...

... warfare ...

... and illnesses.

14.

【原文】

子在齐闻《韶》，三月不知肉味，曰："不图为乐之至于斯也。"

【译文】

孔子在齐国听到帝舜时代的乐曲《韶》，几乎三个月吃肉都不知道味道。于是感叹说："想不到欣赏音乐竟可以到这种境界。"

【English Translation】

Confucius was unable to taste meat for a long time after hearing some Shao music in the state of Qi. Therefore he sighed saying: "I never thought I would become so lost in music to reach this state."

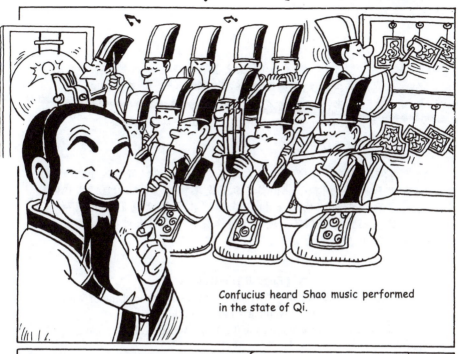

Confucius heard Shao music performed in the state of Qi.

For 3 months thereafter...

This meat is tasteless compared to Shao music.

15.

【原文】

冉有曰:"夫子为卫君乎?"子贡曰:"诺, 吾将问之。"
入, 曰:"伯夷、叔齐何人也?"曰:"古人贤人也。"曰:"怨乎?"
曰:"求仁而得仁, 又何怨?"出曰:"夫子不为也。"

【译文】

冉有问子贡:"老师会为卫君做事吗?"子贡说:"好吧, 等我去问
问他。"子贡进去问孔子:"伯夷、叔齐是怎样的人?"孔子说:"古代的
贤人。"子贡又问:"他们互相怨恨吗?"孔子说:"他们只是想得
到仁德, 而又都得到了, 还怨恨什么呢?"子贡出来对冉有说:"老
师不会为卫君做事的。"

【English Translation】

Ran You asked Zi Gong: "Would teacher assist Prince Ling of Wei?"

Zi Gong answered: "I would ask him about this."

Zi Gong came to Confucius and asked: "What are Bo Yi and Shu Qi like?"

Confucius answered saying: "They were both ancient men of virtue."

Zi Gong asked again: "Did one resent the other after giving up the throne?"

Confucius said: "Since they have succeeded in achieving their only aim, virtue, what could they be resentful about?"

When Zi Gong emerged from Confucius' chambers, he said to Ran You: "Teacher would not serve King Wei."

(Zi Gong made an indirect enquiry of Confucius' feelings towards serving Prince Ling of Wei. The king of Wei was driven into hiding by his father's consort Nan Zi. When the former king of Wei passed away, the throne was inherited by his grandson Kuai Zhe.

When Prince Ling heard news of the passing, he rushed back to Wei and claimed the throne for himself. His action was in direct contrast to that of Bo Yi and Shu Qi, who were known for their insistence that the other had the throne.

By observing Confucius' reaction to this incident, Zi Gong knew that Confucius would not serve Prince Ling of Wei.)

331

16.

【原文】

子曰："饭疏食饮水，曲肱而枕之，乐亦在其中矣。不义而富且贵，于我如浮云。"

【原文】

孔子说："粗茶淡饭，随地而卧，其中也有乐趣。用不正当的方式得来的富贵，对我来说就象浮云一样。"

【English Translation】

Confucius said: "There is joy in eating simply and sleeping anywhere. Illegitimate means of acquiring status and wealth are to me like fleeting clouds."

Joy may be found in coarse food, ...

... plain water, ...

... and arms bent and leaned on as a pillow.

Ill-gotten riches are hollow and to me, like floating clouds.

17.

【原文】

子曰："加我数年,

五十以学《易》,

可以无大过矣。"

【原文】

孔子说:"如果让我多活几年,

到五十岁的时候再学习《易经》,

就不会有大的过错了。"

【English Translation】
Confucius said: "Let me live till fifty and study
The Book of Changes once again. Then I will
not commit any major errors again."

Confucius hoped that he would have more years of study when he was 50, ...

... he would study the *Book of Changes* again and never commit major errors again.

18.

【原文】

子所雅言，《诗》
《书》、执礼，皆雅言也。

【译文】

孔子诵读《诗》、《书》
和赞礼时都用标准的国语。

【English Translation】
The occasions during which Confucius used
correct pronunciaton instead of his Lu dialect
were when reciting the *Book of Poetry*, the *Book
of Documents* and when carrying out the rites.

Confucius always spoke in the Zhou dialect when teaching the Odes and Book of Documents ...

... instead of his native Lu pronunciation.

Don't understand? Good grief!

19.

【原文】

叶公问孔子于子路，子路不对。子曰："女奚不曰，其为人也，发愤忘食，乐以忘忧，不知老之将至云尔。"

【译文】

叶公向子路问孔子的为人，子路不知怎么回答。孔子对子路说："你为什么不说：他的为人，发奋起来就忘记吃饭，快乐起来就忘记忧愁，不晓得衰老将要到来，如此而已。"

【English Translation】

The Duke of Ye asked, to Zi Lu's bafflement, about the personality of Confucius.

Confucius said to Zi Lu: "Why did you not tell him that I'm so intent on enlightenment that I would forget to eat my meals and forget about the encroachment of old age?"

20.

【原文】

子曰："我非生而知之者，
好古，敏以求之者也。"

【译文】

孔子说："我不是生来就有知识的人，
而是因为爱好古代文化，
勤奋而敏捷地去求得知识的人。"

【English Translation】

Confucius said: "I was not born with my knowledge,
but acquired it with my passion for ancient cultures,
with my astuteness and the hard work I put in."

Confucius said he wasn't born with great knowledge.

Due to his keen interest in ancient culture, ...

... he diligently sought information about it.

21.

【原文】
子不语怪,
力，乱，神。

【译文】
孔子从不谈论怪异、
勇力、叛乱和神鬼。

【English Translation】
Confucius never spoke about the paranormal,
feats of strength, disorders in nature or spirits.

Confucius never spoke about monsters, supernatural forces, ...

... the paranormal and spirits.

22.

【原文】

子曰:"三人行, 必有我师焉。择其善者而从之, 其不善者而改之。"

【译文】

孔子说:"几个人一块走路, 其中一定有值得我学习的人。我选择那些优点去学习, 看出那些缺点去改正。"

【English Translation】

Confucius said: "Whenever I travel with other men, there would surely be someone worthy of learning from. By observing them, I would pick out the virtues to emulate and the vices to correct myself in."

Whenever Confucius travelled with others, he looked for something in them worthy of learning.

I must learn that.

He would identify their strengths ...

Mustn't do that.

... and examine himself to see if he had their weaknesses.

23.

【译文】

子曰："天生德于予，
桓魋其如予何！"

【译文】

孔子说："上天赋予我品德，
桓魋能把我怎么样！"

【English Translation】

Confucius said: "My virtues have been bestowed on
me by heaven. What can Huan Kui do to me?"

(NB: Huan Kui is a Song general who
plotted to kill Confucius.)

Note: Huan Kui, a Song Minister of War, had plotted to kill Confucius.

24.

【原文】

子曰:"二三子以我为隐乎? 吾无隐乎尔。吾无行而不与二三子者, 是丘也。"

【译文】

孔子说:"你们这些学生以为我教导你们会有所保留吗? 我不会对你们有所保留的。我没有什么不可以告诉你们的, 这就是我孔丘的为人。"

【English Translation】

Confucius said to his student: "Do you suspect that I am holding back some of my knowledge from you? There is nothing I can keep from you. This is what I, Kong Qiu is like."

25.

【原文】

子以四教：

文，行，忠，信。

【译文】

孔子从四个方面教育学生：

文化知识，社会实践，

忠于国家，信于朋友。

【English Translation】

Confucius educated his students in four disciplines:

the classics, social etiquette, loyalty,

and trust among friends.

Culture,   Conduct,   Loyalty,   Good Faith,

TODAY'S LESSON

These were the 4 subjects Confucius taught.

351

26.

【原文】

子曰："圣人，吾不得而见之矣；得见君子者，斯可矣。"子曰："善人，吾不得而见之矣；得见有恒者，斯可矣。亡而为有，虚而为盈，约而为泰，难乎有恒矣。"

【译文】

孔子说："圣人，我不指望看见了；能看见君子，也就可以了。"又说："善人，我不指望看见了；能看见有操守的人，也就可以了。本来没有假装有，本来空虚假装充实，本来穷困假装富有，这样的人，只怕连操守也没有了。"

【English Translation】

Confucius : "I do not hope to meet a sage face to face. The most that I can hope for is to meet a true gentleman."

Again he said: "A faultless man I cannot hope to meet. The most I can hope for is to meet a man of principles.

I see the shallow pretending to be men of substance, the improvident pretending to be affluent, even a man of principles will not be easy to find."

27.

【原文】
子钓而不网，
弋不射宿。

【译文】
孔子钓鱼不用网，
射猎不射归巢的鸟。

【English Translation】
When Confucius fished, he used a line and
not a net. When he went fowling,
he did not shoot roosting birds.

Confucius only fished
with hooks and not nets.

He never shot at
a sitting target.

28.

【原文】

子曰:"盖有不知而作之者,我无是也。多闻,择其善者而从之;多见而识之;知之次也。"

【译文】

孔子说:"不懂装懂的毛病我没有。我主张多听各种意见,选择其中好的来学习;多看各种事情,使自己认识广泛。而先知是次要的。"

【English Translation】

Confucius said: "I do not pretend to know what I do not. I advocate listening to all sorts of opinions and picking the beneficial from all these to practise. Exposing oneself to all categories of knowledge would broaden one's knowledge base. Understanding acquired in this way is reliable but it is not as good as innate knowledge."

Instead of pretending to know a lot, be receptive to all sorts of knowledge so as to find something sound to learn.

This is a reliable way to acquire knowledge.

357

29.

【原文】

互乡难与言，童子见，门人惑。子曰："与其进也，不与其退也，唯何甚！人洁己以进，与其洁也，不保其往也。"

【译文】

互乡是个野蛮的地方，但那里的一个少年却得到孔子的接见，弟子们迷惑不解。孔子说："我赞成他们的进步，不赞成他们的落后，凡事不可太过分，人家既然改正缺点以求进步，就应该赞赏他们的改进，不要老看人家过去的污点。"

【English Translation】

Although Hu village was a barbaric region, Confucius received a youth who came from that place in order to see him. This surprised his students. Confucius said: "I approve of their coming but not what they do when they leave. Since he came with the intentions of improving himself, one should support him and not take his background against him."

To the disciple's surprise, Confucius accepted a disciple from the Hu tribe.

I support their progress, not regression.

Since they realize their position and wish to improve, we shouldn't keep harping on their past.

30.

【原文】

子曰:"仁远乎哉?

我欲仁,斯仁至矣。"

【译文】

孔子说:"仁德很遥远吗?

只要想达到仁德,仁德就会向你靠近。"

【English Translation】

Confucius said: "Is benevolence really very distant from us? We can reach it if we truly yearn for it."

31.

【原文】

陈司败问："昭公知礼乎?"孔子曰："知礼。"孔子退，揖巫马期而进之，曰："吾闻君子不党，君子亦党乎？君取于吴，为同姓，谓之吴孟子。君而知礼，孰不知礼?"巫马期以告。子曰："丘也幸，苟有过，人必知之。"

【译文】

陈司败问孔子："鲁昭公懂礼吗?"孔子回答："懂礼。"孔子走了以后，陈司败请巫马期走近自己，说："我听说君子无所偏袒，难道君子也偏袒吗？鲁昭公从吴国娶了一位夫人，鲁和吴是同姓，依礼是不能通婚的，所以称为吴孟子而不叫吴姬。如果鲁昭公算懂礼的话，还有谁不懂礼呢?"巫马期把这话告诉了孔子。孔子说："我很幸运，如果有错误，别人一定指出来。"

【English Translation】

Chen Si Bai asked Confucius: "Did Duke Zhao of Lu know the rites? "

Confucius answered: "Yes, he did."

After Confucius left, Chen Si Bai summoned Wu Ma Qi to his side and said: "Is it not true that gentlemen must be impartial at all times? Duke Zhao of Lu was married to a lady of Wu. Lu and Wu branched out from the same clan and the rites prohibit marriage between those of the same clan. That is the reason Duke Zhao's wife was called Wu Meng Zi and not Wu Ji. If Duke Lu is counted as one who practises the rites, who can we consider as one who does not know the rites?"

Wu Ma Qi reported all this to Confucius who replied: "I am very fortunate to have someone point out my errors when I commit one."

32.

【原文】

子与人歌而善，
必使反之，而后和之。

【译文】

孔子和别人一道唱歌，
有唱得好的，就一定
要求人家再唱一遍，
然后再跟着唱。

【English Translation】

When anyone sang in the presence of Confucius
a song that he liked, he never joined in at once but
asked for it to be repeated and then joined in.

33.

【原文】

子曰:"文,莫吾犹人也。
躬行君子,则吾未之有得。"

【译文】

孔子说:"书本上的知识,
我已经学得差不多了。但要做
一个身体力行的君子,我还没有做到。"

【English Translation】

Confucius said: "I have almost mastered the
knowledge in the books. But as regards to carrying
out the duties of a gentleman in real life, I have not
had a chance yet to show what I could do."

367

34.

【原文】

子曰:"若圣与仁,则吾岂敢!抑为之不厌,诲人不倦,则可谓云尔已矣。"公西华曰:"正唯弟子不能学也。"

【译文】

孔子说:"如果说我是圣人和仁人,我哪里敢当!我只不过是不懈的学习和工作,教诲别人不知疲倦,就不过如此而已。"公西华说:"这正是我们学不到。"

【English Translation】

Confucius said: "I would not dare to accept the title of sage or man of benevolence. I have merely not slackened in work or learning. Neither do I tire of teaching others."

Gong Xi Hua said after hearing this: "It is exactly this that we cannot achieve."

Confucius did not consider himself a sage or a man of benevolence.

Today's Lesson

But merely an untiring learner and enthusiastic teacher.

That's exactly what we failed to do.

You flatter me.

35.

【原文】

子疾病，子路请祷。子曰："有诸？"子路对曰："有之。《诔》曰：'祷尔于上下神祇。'"子曰："丘之祷久矣。"

【译文】

孔子病得很重，子路请求向鬼神祈祷。孔子问："有这样的事吗？"子路回答说："有的，《诔》文说：'为你向天神地祇祈祷。'孔子说："那我早就祷告过了。"

【English Translation】

Zi Lu asked to intercede with the gods and spirits, on behalf of Confucius, when the latter was chronically ill. When Confucius heard this he questioned Zi Lu: "Did you really make this request?"

Zi Lu answered: "Yes I did. *The Book of Eulogies* suggests this: 'Pray to the gods from above and below for you.' "

Confucius said: "What justifies me in the eyes of Heaven is the life I have led. There is no need for any rite now."

Note: The Eulogies suggest that the effectiveness of prayer is based on one's merits. Confucius, being virtuous had been praying for a long time.

36.

【原文】

子曰:"奢则不孙, 俭则固。

与其不孙也, 宁固。"

【译文】

孔子说:"奢侈豪华就不谦,

俭省朴素就显得简陋。

与其不谦, 宁可简陋。"

【English Translation】

Confucius said: "Just as lavish living leads to snobbishness, frugality leads to shabbiness. But of the two, it is better to be shabby."

37.

【原文】

子曰:"君子坦荡荡,
小人长戚戚。"

【译文】

孔子说:"君子心中坦荡踏实,
小人时常忧心忡忡。"

【English Translation】

Confucius said: "A gentleman is calm and at
ease while a petty man is fretful and ill at ease."

A gentleman is always magnanimous.

They must be bad-mouthing me.

A petty man is always emotional and burdened with anxiety.

38.

【原文】

子温而厉，威而不猛，
恭而安。

【译文】

孔子温和又严厉，
有威仪而不凶狠，
庄重而平静。

【English Translation】
Confucius was gentle yet firm, commanding
but not harsh, grave but calm.

GATEWAY TO CHINESE CLASSICAL LITERATURE

Chinese classical literature encompasses a dazzling range, from poetry, rhymed prose, essays to drama and novels. Despite the passage of time, these works remain fresh and relevant today. Using illustrations and lucid exposition of the various styles of classical Chinese literature, this book takes the reader on a tour of the Chinese literary world, at the same time affording valuable insights into the themes and social issues of early Chinese civilisation.

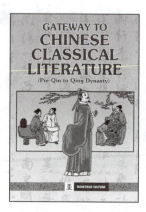

POPULAR CHINESE PROVERBS

Popular Chinese Proverbs collects several old favourites and some of the most widely used expressions. Using vibrant illustrations and clear explanations of the metaphors and history behind them, their origins and meanings are presented in an easy-to-understand format.

THE ART OF PEACE: PRACTICAL TEACHINGS OF MO ZI

During the chaotic Warring States Period (475 – 221 BC), when China was divided into numerous small states locked in endless conflict and power struggle, philosopher Mo Zi spread his message of peace and universal love.

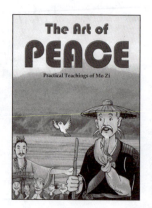

CHINESE CULTURE SERIES
150x210mm, fully illustrated

ORIGINS OF CHINESE PEOPLE AND CUSTOMS
Explores the beginnings of the Chinese people, origins of Chinese names, Chinese zodiac signs, the afterlife, social etiquette and more!

ORIGINS OF CHINESE FESTIVALS
Stories about Lunar New Year, Chinese Valentine's Day, Qing Ming, Dragon Boat, Zhong Yuan, Mid-Autumn Festivals and more.

ORIGINS OF CHINESE MUSIC AND ART
Interesting facts about the "Four Treasures of the Study": the brush, ink, paper and inkstone, which form the cornerstone of Chinese culture.

ORIGINS OF CHINESE FOLK ARTS
Packed with useful information on artistic interests covering Chinese embroidery, lacquerware, paper cutting, face masks and pottery.

ORIGINS OF CHINESE MARTIAL ARTS
Traces the origins of the *gongfu* of Shaolin and Wudang warriors and their philosophy and chivalry code.

ORIGINS OF CHINESE CUISINE
Showcases famous and best-relished dishes, including Peking Roast Duck and Buddha Jumps Over the Wall, and the stories behind them.

ORIGINS OF CHINESE FOOD CULTURE
Covers the origins, history, customs, and the art and science of Chinese food culture, including the 18 methods of cooking.

ORIGINS OF CHINESE TEA AND WINE
Tea and wine have a long history in China. In fact, both have become firmly entrenched in the culture and customs of the Chinese people.

ORIGINS OF CHINESE SCIENCE & TECHNOLOGY
Covers great inventions by the Chinese: the compass, paper-making, gunpowder and printing. Also explores Chinese expertise in the fields of geography, mathematics, agriculture and astronomy.

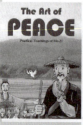

《论语》全集

第一集

绘画 ：萧成材

翻译（白话）：徐晖

翻译（英文）：谢维万

亚太图书有限公司出版